SUMMON'S
BIBLE MISCELLANY

SUMMON'S
BIBLE MISCELLANY

Parminder Summon

WILLIAM B. EERDMANS PUBLISHING COMPANY
GRAND RAPIDS, MICHIGAN / CAMBRIDGE, U.K.

First published 2006 in the United Kingdom by
the Canterbury Press Norwich
(a publishing imprint of
Hymns Ancient & Modern Limited,
a registered charity)
9–17 St Albans Place, London N1 0NX

This edition published 2006 in the United States of America by
Wm. B. Eerdmans Publishing Co.
2140 Oak Industrial Drive N.E., Grand Rapids, Michigan 49505 /
P.O. Box 163, Cambridge CB3 9PU U.K.
www.eerdmans.com

Printed in the United States of America

11 10 09 08 07 06   7 6 5 4 3 2 1

ISBN-10 0-8028-3390-X
ISBN-13 978-0-8028-3390-7

CONTENTS

ACKNOWLEDGEMENTS

Many thanks to the team at SCM-Canterbury Press, particularly Christine Smith and Mary Matthews for their encouragement.

Every effort has been made to trace and acknowledge copyright owners for material used in this book. We apologize for any inadvertent omissions or errors. Please contact us to report such errors and we will ensure full acknowledgement in the future.

INTRODUCTION

The Bible is the most influential collection of books in human history. It is without parallel in its ability to guide and inspire individuals, families, tribes and nations. Thousands have given their lives to preserve the eternal truths of the Book of Books. There are more copies of the Bible than any other book and it is the most translated work of any age with versions in over 2,100 languages. More than 60 million copies of the Bible are sold every year and it remains far and away the most popular book ever.

Every reader, regardless of circumstances, can find a personal message, in the Bible. From explanations of how the universe came into being to simple words for children, the Bible contains the whole range of universal experience. It is the oracle of oracles, the wisdom of all wisdom, the power of all power. Kingdoms have fallen or been secured because of the Bible. It claims to judge every one of us, penetrating our hearts and judging our thoughts and attitudes.

The Bible makes extraordinary claims about itself. It claims to be supernatural, eternal, a remedy against sin, a source of strength and a light to our path.

The primary purpose of this book, therefore, is to direct you to the Bible, to read, meditate and apply its timeless guidance. For it is a sad fact, that although the Bible is revered in many cultures, umpteen people in the so-called 'developed world' are neglecting its wisdom. This is in contrast to the developing world where the hunger for the Bible continues to grow at an amazing pace.

I hope this book is a useful guide to encourage exploration of the Bible as it contains a diverse range of curious facts, interesting people and entertaining information about the Bible.

For Les, Alison, Samuel and Jonathan Howard

The grass withers and the flowers fall,
but the word of our God stands forever.

Isaiah 40.8

WHY READ THE BIBLE?

The Bible contains:
the mind of god
the state of man
the way of salvation and the happiness of believers
light to direct
food to nurture
comfort to cheer.
It is:
the traveller's map
the pilgrim's staff
the pilot's compass
the soldier's sword and the Christian's charter.
It is:
a mine of wealth
a paradise of glory and a river of pleasure.
Its doctrines are holy.
Its precepts are binding.
Its histories are true.
Its wisdom is immutable.
It should rule the heart,
fill the mind and guide the feet.
It is given to us in life,
will be opened at the Judgement,
and is the Word of God that stands forever.

Anon

SHAKESPEARE'S BIBLE CODE?

There has been growing interest over many years about possible 'secret' messages in the Bible. While the Bible is best read as an open book, many people have tried to determine whether the Bible's structure contains more than its words. In this context, it is interesting that William Shakespeare is thought to have helped with the translation of the King James Bible.

The King James Bible, or Authorized Version, was completed in 1611 when Shakespeare was aged 46. Psalm 46 is intriguing for its 46th word is 'shake' and 46 words before the end, we find the word 'spear'. So, Shakespeare may have had a hand in the translation of the King James Bible, but this tenuous link is the only indication of it.

BIBLE FACTS

King James

Category	Bible
Books	66
Longest book	Psalms
Middle book(s)	Micah and Nahum
Shortest book	2 John
Chapters	1,189
Longest chapter	Psalm 119
Middle chapter	Psalm 117
Shortest chapter	Psalm 117
Verses	31,101
Longest verse	Esther 8.9
Middle verse(s)	Psalm 118.8
Shortest verse	John 11.35
Words	783,137
Letters	3,566,480

AND FIGURES

Bible Statistics

Old Testament	New Testament
39	27
Psalms	Luke
Proverbs	2 Thessalonians
Obadiah	2 John
929	260
Psalm 119	Luke 1
Job 29	Romans 13
Psalm 117	2 John
23,114	7,987
Esther 8.9	Revelation 20.4
2 Chronicles 20.17, 18	Acts 27.17
1 Chronicles 1.25	John 11.35
602,585	180,552
2,278,100	1,288,380

The word 'Bible' simply means a collection of books. It was originally made up of books written in three languages: Hebrew, Aramaic and Koine Greek.

Division of the Bible

Cardinal Hugo de S. Caro introduced a system of chapters in AD 1238. Stephen Langton (*c.*1150–1228), an Archbishop of Canterbury, is believed to be the first person to divide the whole Bible into defined *chapters* at the University of Paris.

Hugh of St Cher introduced chapter divisions in 1244. The Hebrew Old Testament was divided into verses by Rabbi Nathan around 1448. Dots previously marked verse divisions. These were standardized (but not numbered) by the Masoretes in about the year AD 900.

Robert Estienne (1503–59), a Paris printer who like so many people involved in Bible translation or printing had to flee from persecution, introduced the *verse* divisions now in use when he was a refugee in Geneva, Switzerland, in 1551. This was in a Latin and Greek New Testament. The first New Testament in English to contain these verse divisions was the Geneva Version of 1560. Legend has it that the numbering was done in a moving carriage. This might account for uneven verse length, mid-sentence division in some cases, and a general impression of lack of planning, but there is no firm evidence to support the legend.

The first English Bible translation was initiated by John Wyclif in 1382 and completed by John Purvey in 1388.

It takes about 70 hours to read the entire Bible.

About 170,000 Bibles are distributed each day in the USA.

Moses wrote the most books in the Old Testament. He wrote the first five books of the Bible, referred to as the Pentateuch, the foundation of the Bible.

The Apostle Paul wrote the most books in the New Testament.

His inspired work comprises 14 books (over half) of the New Testament.

Many scholars agree that Job is the oldest book in the Bible, written by an unknown Israelite about 1500 BC. Others hold that the Pentateuch (the first five books of the Bible) are the oldest books in the Bible, written between 1446 and 1406 BC.

By contrast, the book of Malachi, written about 400 BC, is the most recent book in the Old Testament.

The book of James, written as early as AD 45, is probably the oldest book in the New Testament. The book of revelation is the most recent New Testament book, written around AD 90.

A Bible in the University of Göttingen is written on 2,470 palm leaves.

There are 8,674 different Hebrew words in the Bible, 5,624 different Greek words, and 12,143 different English words in the King James Version.

The Bible is big business. In the last 40 years alone the eight new Bible versions published in English have sold well in excess of 100 million copies. Worldwide sales of the Good News Bible (1976) stand at over 7 million; the New English Bible (1970) has sold over 10 million; about 23 million copies of the Living Bible have been bought since 1971; and sales of the New International Version topped a million copies within less than a year of its publication date in 1979. Even King James's allegedly outdated Authorized Version of 1611 still brings in every year over a million pounds in revenue for its publishers. The Bible is without doubt the world's best-selling book.

St Jerome, writing in the fourth century, described the completed Bible as the 'Divine library', thus recognizing that its multiple parts had a single, divine source. Even earlier, Origen is on record as having this to say: 'There are many sacred writings, yet there is but one Book. All the writings breathe the spirit of fullness, and there is nothing, whether in the Law or in the Prophets, in the Evangelists or the apostles, which does not descend from the fullness of the Divine Majesty.'

THE DISCO PSALM

Psalm 137 is a remarkable song recalling Israel's exile in Babylon. It is the only Psalm recorded by three artists – Don McLean (1971), Bob Marley (1983) and the disco band, Boney M. These are the lyrics of the Boney M version that reached number one in the UK in April 1978.

By the rivers of Babylon, there we sat down
ye-eah we wept, when we remembered Zion.
By the rivers of Babylon, there we sat down
ye-eah we wept, when we remembered Zion.
When the wicked
Carried us away in captivity
Required from us a song
Now how shall we sing the lord's song in a strange land
When the wicked
Carried us away in captivity
Requiring of us a song
Now how shall we sing the lord's song in a strange land
Let the words of our mouth and the meditations of our heart
be acceptable in thy sight here tonight
Let the words of our mouth and the meditation of our hearts
be acceptable in thy sight here tonight
By the rivers of Babylon, there we sat down
ye-eah we wept, when we remembered Zion.
By the rivers of Babylon, there we sat down
ye-eah we wept, when we remembered Zion.
By the rivers of Babylon (Dark tears of Babylon)
there we sat down (You got to sing a song)
ye-eah we wept (Sing a song of love)
when we remember Zion. (Yeah yeah yeah yeah yeah)
By the rivers of Babylon (Rough bits of Babylon)
there we sat down (You hear the people cry)
ye-eah we wept (They need that)
when we remember Zion. (Ooh, have the power)

SAYING GRACE

Scripture commends the practice of giving thanks for our food and drink, as recorded Deuteronomy 8.10: 'When you have eaten and are satisfied, praise the LORD your God for the good land he has given you.'

Here are some examples of notable graces:

God is great, and God is good,
And we thank him for our food;
By his hand we all are fed;
Give us, Lord, our daily bread.

Lord Jesus be drink and food.

Martin Luther

Some have hunger, but no meat;
Some have meat, but no hunger;
I have both.
God be praised!

Oliver Cromwell

Good Lord – Bless these sinners as they eat their dinners.
Amen.

For Bacon, Eggs and Buttered Toast,
Praise Father, Son and Holy Ghost.

A German blessing

Alles das wir haben,	All that we have,
Alles ist gegaben.	is all a gift.
Es kommt, O Gott, von dir,	It comes, O God, from you;
Wir danken dir dafuer.	We thank you for it.

Versicle and Response (Psalm 145.16–17):

V: The eyes of all wait upon you, O Lord,
R: and you give them their food in due season.

[7]

V: You open wide your hand
R: and satisfy the needs of every living creature.
Gloria Patri (Glory to the Father, and to the Son, and to the Holy Spirit. As it was in the beginning, is now, and will be forever. Amen.)

A Spanish Blessing

Cristo, pan de vida,   Christ, bread of life,
Ven y bendice esta comida.   Come and bless this food.
Amen.   Amen

Jewish Blessing

We praise You, O Lord and God, King of the Universe, Creator
    of the fruit of the vine.
We praise You, O Lord and God, King of the Universe, bringer
    of bread from the Earth.

To the tune of 'Edelweiss' from *The Sound of Music*

Bless our friends,
Bless our food,
Come, O Lord and sit with us.

May our talk
Glow with peace;
Come with your love to surround us.

Friendship and love
May they bloom and glow,
Bloom and glow forever.

Bless our friends,
Bless our food,
Bless all mankind forever.

The 'Selkirk Grace' by Robert Burns

Some hae meat and canna eat,
And some would eat that want it;
But we hae meat, and we can eat,
Sae let the Lord be thankit.

Some have meat and cannot eat;
Some cannot eat that want it:
But we have meat and we can eat
Sae let the Lord be thankit!

For the very hungry:
Ta, Pa. Amen.

THE IMPORTANCE OF THE SABBATH

Sabbath – (Heb. v. shabbath) *meaning 'to rest from labour',
the day of rest.*

Originated by God in man's innocence – Genesis 2.3: And God
blessed the seventh day, and made it holy, because on it he
rested from all the work of creating that he had done.

Hallowed: Exodus 20.11: For in six days the LORD made the
heavens and the earth, the sea, and all that is in them, but
he rested on the seventh day. Therefore the LORD blessed the
Sabbath day, and made it *holy* (hallowed it).

Sanctified: Exodus 31.15: For six days work is to be done, but
the seventh day is a Sabbath of rest, *holy* to the LORD.

Commanded to be kept: Deuteronomy 5.15: Therefore the
LORD your God has *commanded* you to observe the Sabbath
day.

Sign of God's blessing: Exodus 23.12: This will be a sign

between me and you for the generations to come, so that you may know that I am the LORD who makes you holy.

Blessing upon those who keep the Sabbath: Isaiah 56.2: *Blessed* are those that do this, those who hold it fast, who keep the Sabbath without desecrating it, and keep their hands from doing any evil.

Denunciation against those who profane the Sabbath: Nehemiah 13.18: Didn't your ancestors do the same things, so that our God brought all this calamity upon us, and upon this city? Now you are stirring up more wrath against Israel by *desecrating* the Sabbath.

Sign of eternal rest: Hebrews 4.9: There remains, then a *Sabbath-rest* for the people of God.

Jesus is the Lord of the Sabbath: Mark 2.28: So the Son of man is *Lord* even of the Sabbath.

TaNaKh – THE HEBREW BIBLE

Though non-Jews commonly use the word 'Bible' and 'Old Testament', the appropriate term to use for the Hebrew scriptures is the acronym *TaNaKh*. This word is derived from the Hebrew letters of its three components:

Torah: The Books of Genesis (*Bereshit*), Exodus (*Shemot*), Leviticus (*Vayikrah*), Numbers (*Bamidbar*) and Deuteronomy (*Devarim*).

Nevi'im (Prophets): The Books of Joshua, Judges, 1 Samuel, 2 Samuel, 1 Kings, 2 Kings, Isaiah, Jeremiah, Ezekiel, Hosea, Joel, Amos, Obadiah, Jonah, Micah, Nahum, Habukkuk, Zephaniah, Haggai, Zechariah and Malachi. (The last twelve are sometimes grouped together as '*Trei Asar*' ['Twelve'].)

Ketuvim (Writings): The Books of Psalms, Proverbs, Job, Song of Songs, Ruth, Lamentations, Ecclesiastes, Esther, most of

Daniel, Ezra and Nehemiah, 1 Chronicles and 2 Chronicles. Samuel (Shmuel), Kings (Melachim) and Chronicles (*Divrei hayamim*) are divided into two parts in Christian Scripture because originally the printers decided they were too big to be issued as single volumes – thus the titles of Volume 1 and Volume 2 were attached to them.

Many Christian Bibles have expanded versions of several of some of these books (for example, Esther, Ezra, Daniel, Jeremiah and Chronicles) including extra material that is not accepted as canonical in Judaism. Jews regard the additional material as apocryphal. Jesus referred to the complete TaNaKh in Matthew 23.55 when he spoke about the death of Abel (at the beginning of the TaNaKh), and the death of Zechariah (at the end of the TaNaKh).

Listed below are the books of the TaNaKh according to their major divisions. Additionally the Prophets section is sub-divided into the Former Prophets and the Latter Prophets. The Latter Prophets also include 'The Twelve' (Minor Prophets).

The Torah
Genesis
Exodus
Leviticus
Numbers
Deuteronomy

The Prophets – The Former Prophets

Joshua	Samuel
Judges	Kings

The Prophets – The Latter Prophets

Isaiah	Amos	Habakkuk
Jeremiah	Obadiah	Zephaniah
Ezekiel	Jonah	Haggai
Hosea	Micah	Zechariah
Joel	Nahum	Malachi

The Writings

Psalms	Ecclesiastes
Proverbs	Esther
Job	Daniel
Song of Solomon	Ezra-Nehemiah
Ruth	Chronicles
Lamentations	

The order of the Hebrew Bible and Protestant Old Testament is like this:

TaNaKh	Old Testament
Genesis	Genesis
Exodus	Exodus
Leviticus	Leviticus
Numbers	Numbers
Deuteronomy	Deuteronomy
Joshua	Joshua
Judges	Judges
Samuel	Ruth
Kings	1 Samuel
Isaiah	2 Samuel
Jeremiah	1 Kings
Ezekiel	2 Kings
Hosea	1 Chronicles
Joel	2 Chronicles
Amos	Ezra
Obadiah	Nehemiah

TaNaKh	Old Testament
Jonah	Esther
Micah	Job
Nahum	Psalms
Habakkuk	Proverbs
Zephaniah	Ecclesiastes
Haggai	Song of Solomon
Zechariah	Isaiah
Malachi	Jeremiah
Psalms	Lamentations
Proverbs	Ezekiel
Job	Daniel
Song of Solomon	Hosea
Ruth	Joel
Lamentations	Amos
Ecclesiastes	Obadiah
Esther	Jonah
Daniel	Micah
Ezra-Nehemiah	Nahum
Chronicles	Habakkuk
	Zephaniah
	Haggai
	Zechariah
	Malachi

BIBLE DIETS

The Bible has many things to say about eating sensibly and in our modern age, those eager to promote healthy living have seized upon any 'biblical' nutrition tips. Concerns over obesity and media coverage of health problems associated with being overweight have led to hundreds of different diet plans.

Three such plans seek to portray biblical advice on dieting and good health as their unique selling points. They are:

The Bible Diet

Promoted by Dr Rex Russell since 1996, *The Bible Diet* has three key principles:

1. *Eat the foods God created for you.* Going back to creation, these foods are 'every seed-bearing plant on the face of the whole earth and every tree that has fruit with seed in it' (Genesis 1.29). Also included are 'fine flour, olive oil and honey I gave you to eat' (Ezekiel 16.19) and food eaten by Jesus, such as fishes and loaves.
2. *Don't alter God's design* – try to stick to natural foods (Ezekiel 47.12).
3. *Don't let any food or drink become your God* – exercise self control, 'put a knife to your throat if you are given to gluttony' (Proverbs 23.2).

www.biblediet.net

The Maker's Diet

Promoted by Jordan S. Rubin since 2000, *The Maker's Diet* 'pays special attention to the three 'I's that contribute to exceptional health', namely:

- Balancing *insulin* to enhance mood and sharpen concentration
- Reducing *infection* to minimize the burden on the body's immune system

- Managing *inflammation* by reducing aches and pains

Appropriately, the Maker's Diet is a 40-day programme to achieve and maintain your ideal body weight, reduce stress on the immune system and ensure mental, emotional and physical health.

www.makersdiet.com

The Weigh Down Diet

More controversially, American dietitian Gwen Shamblin has been promoting the *Weigh Down Diet* since 1986. Critics claim Shamblin also promotes unbiblical views of the Trinity and her approach cannot, therefore, be in line with Scripture. However, Shamblin advises her supporters to stick within 'God's perfect boundaries of hunger and fullness' if they want to lose weight. 'Head hunger' – the urge to eat when the body is not calling for it – is not a physiological urge, but rather spiritual hunger. The Weigh Down programme is delivered through a series of hour-long 'workshops' designed to 'change the heart and your own desire' rather than the foods you eat. Thus you eat less, because you only eat enough to satisfy your hunger. Through submitting our wills, we become more aware of God's plans for us and experience greater desire for him rather than food.

www.wdworkshop.com

DIVISIONS OF PSALMS

The songbook of the Bible has five divisions, perhaps to mirror the five books of the Torah – Genesis, Exodus, Leviticus, Numbers and Deuteronomy.

Book	Psalms	Author	Torah Connection	Characteristics
Book 1	1–41	Almost all David	Genesis – concerning man	Mostly individual laments
Book 2	42–72	Mostly David, the sons of Korah and Asaph	Exodus – concerning Israel	Mostly temple liturgies
Book 3	73–89	Mostly the sons of Korah	Leviticus – concerning worship	Mostly group laments and temple liturgies
Book 4	90–106	Almost all by unknown authors	Numbers – concerning Israel and the nations of the earth	Prayers and new songs
Book 5	107–150	Mostly David	Deuteronomy – concerning God and his word	Blessings for Israel and the earth

Each book concludes with a *doxology*, or a praise, to God, usually found within the last verse, or two, of the final Psalm in the division. In the case of Book 5, Psalm 150, in its entirety, is a 'concluding' doxology.

TWENTY-ONE STATES OF MAN WITHOUT GOD

1. Alienated from God (Ephesians 4.18)
2. Blind (John 12.40; 2 Corinthians 4.4; 1 John 2.11)
3. Carnally or fleshly minded (Romans 8.6, 13)
4. Corrupt (Matthew 7.17–18; 1 Timothy 6.5)
5. Darkened (Matthew 6.23; John 3.19; Romans 1.21; Ephesians 4.18; 1 John 1.6–7)
6. Dead in sin (John 5.24; Romans 8.6; Colossians 2.13; 1 Timothy 5.6; 1 John 3.14)
7. Deceived (Titus 3.3)
8. Defiled or filthy (Isaiah 64.6; Titus 1.15; 2 Peter 2.20; Revelation 22.11)
9. Disobedient (Matthew 7.23; Ephesians 2.3; Titus 3.3)
10. An enemy of God (James 4.4)
11. Evil (Matthew 6.22; 12.33–34; John 3.20)
12. Foolish (Matthew 7.26; Ephesians 5.15; Titus 3.3)
13. Hateful (Titus 3.3)
14. Hypocritical (Matthew 6.2, 5, 16; 23.13, 29)
15. Malicious and envious (Titus 3.3)
16. Proud (Romans 1.30; 1 Timothy 6.4; 2 Timothy 3.4; James 4.6; 1 Peter 5.5)
17. Rejecting truth (2 Timothy 4.4)
18. Lovers of self (2 Timothy 3.2)
19. A slave of sin (John 8.34; Romans 6.16–17, 20; Titus 3.3)
20. Unconscious of bondage (John 8.33; Romans 7.7)
21. Unrighteous (1 Corinthians 6.9; Revelation 22.11)

TWELVE TESTS OF ABRAHAM

Abraham's faith was tested at least twelve specific times. Some of them were not what we might call big tests, but together they establish a picture of Abraham as a person whose faith was genuine. After the last of these, God said, 'Now I know that you fear God, because you have not withheld from me your son, your only son' (Genesis 22.12). Abraham's tests also have applications for us today.

1. *Genesis 12.1–7*
Test: Abraham left Ur and Haran for an unknown destination at God's direction.
Application: Do we trust God with our future?

2. *Genesis 13.8–13*
Test: Abraham directed a peaceful separation from Lot and settled at the oaks of Mamre.
Application: Do we trust God with our interests even when we seem to be receiving an unfair settlement?

3. *Genesis 14.13–16*
Test: Abraham rescued Lot from the five kings.
Application: Does our faithfulness to others bear witness to trust in God's faithfulness?

4. *Genesis 14.17–24*
Test: Abraham gave a tithe of loot to the godly king of Salem, Melchizedek, and refused the gift of the king of Sodom.
Application: Do we give proper honour to God and refuse to receive honour that belongs to him?

5. *Genesis 15.1–6*
Test: Abraham trusted God's promise that he would have a son.
Application: Do we have faith that God will fulfil his promises to us?

6. *Genesis 15.7–16*
Test: Abraham received the promised land by faith, though the fulfilment would not come for many generations.
Application: How do we demonstrate continued trust in God when required to wait?

7. *Genesis 17.9–27*
Test: At God's command, Abraham circumcised every male in his family.
Application: Do we act simply in obedience to God, regardless of whether we understand the significance of what we are asked to do?

8. *Genesis 18.1–8*
Test: Abraham welcomed strangers, who turned out to be angels.
Application: Do we practise hospitality?

9. *Genesis 18.22–33*
Test: Abraham prayed for Sodom.
Application: Do we offer compassion or condemnation?

10. *Genesis 20.1–17*
Test: Abraham admitted to wrongdoing and took the actions needed to set things right.
Application: Do we tend to cover up, or confess?

11. *Genesis 21.22–34*
Test: Abraham negotiated a treaty with Abimelech concerning a well.
Application: Can people depend on our words and promises?

12. *Genesis 22.1–12*
Test: Abraham was prepared to sacrifice his son Isaac.
Application: Do we demonstrate faith in God no matter what?

Source unknown

CATEGORIES OF ANGELS

Archai: rulers (1 Corinthians 15.24; Ephesians 1.21)
Exousiai: authorities (1 Corinthians 15.24; Ephesians 1.21)
Dunameis: powers (1 Corinthians 15.24; Ephesians 1.21)
Kuriotes: dominions (Ephesians 1.21; Colossians 1.16)
Thronoi: thrones (Colossians 1.16)
Archontes: leaders, princes (1 Corinthians 2.6)
Kosmokratores: world rulers (Ephesians 6.12)

THE BOOK OF ISAIAH MIRRORS THE BIBLE

The book of Isaiah is constructed much like the entire Bible. Consider the similarities:

Bible: 66 books.
Isaiah: 66 chapters.

Bible: First 39 books mainly concern Israel.
Isaiah: First 39 chapters mainly concern Israel.

Bible: Last 27 books concern the life and coming of Jesus Christ.
Isaiah: Last 27 chapters concern the life and coming of Jesus Christ.

WHAT IS SIN?

Man calls it an accident,
God calls it abomination.

Man calls it a defect,
God calls it a disease.

Man calls it an error,
God calls it an enmity.

Man calls it a liberty,
God calls it lawlessness.

Man calls it a trifle,
God calls it a tragedy.

Man calls it a mistake,
God calls it a madness.

Man calls it a weakness,
God calls it wilfulness.

Source unknown

THE BOOKS OF THE BIBLE POEM

In Genesis the world was made by God's creative hand;
In Exodus the Hebrews march to gain the Promised Land;
Leviticus contains the Law, holy, just and good,
Numbers records the tribes enrolled, all sons of Abraham's
    blood.
Moses in Deuteronomy records God's mighty deeds.
Brave Joshua into Canaan's land the host of Israel leads.
In Judges their rebellion oft provokes the Lord to smite.
But Ruth records the faith of one well pleasing in his sight.
In 1st and 2nd Samuel of Jesse's son we read;
Ten tribes in 1st and 2nd Kings revolted from his seed.
In 1st and 2nd Chronicles we see Judah captive made,
But Ezra leads the remnant back by princely Cyrus' aid.
The city walls of Zion Nehemiah builds again,

While Esther saves her people from the plots of wicked men.
In Job we read how faith will live beneath afflictions' rod,
And David's Psalms are precious songs to every child of
  God.
The Proverbs, like a goodly string of choicest pearls,
  appear;
Ecclesiastes teaches men how vain are all things here.
The Song of Solomon exalts sweet Sharon's lovely rose,
While Christ the Saviour and the King the rapt Isaiah
  shows.
The admonishing Jeremiah apostate Israel warns,
His plaintive Lamentations their awful downfall mourns.
Ezekiel tells in wondrous words the Kingdom's mysteries,
While God's great Kingdom yet to come Daniel in vision
  sees.
Of judgement and of mercy Hosea loves to tell,
Joel describes the blessed days when God with man will
  dwell.
Among Tekoa's herdmen Amos received his call,
And Obadiah prophesies of Edom's final fall.
Jonah enshrines a wondrous type of Christ, our risen Lord;
Micah pronounces Judah lost – lost but to be restored.
Nahum declares on Nineveh just judgement shall be
  poured
When Christ our risen Saviour shall come to be adored.
A view of Chaldees' coming doom Habakkuk's vision gives,
While Zephaniah warns the Jews to turn, repent and live.
Haggai wrote to those who saw the Temple built again,
Zechariah prophesies of Christ's triumphant reign.
Malachi was the last to touch that high prophetic cord;
His final notes sublimely show the coming of the Lord.
Matthew, Mark, Luke and John the Gospel story give,
Describing how the Saviour was born and died that man
  may live.
Acts tells how well the apostles preached with signs in
  every place,
And Paul in Romans proves that man is saved through
  faith by grace.

The Apostle in Corinthians instructs, exhorts, reproves;
Galatians proves that faith in Christ alone the Father
approves.
Ephesians and Philippians tell what Christians ought to be;
Colossians bids us live for God and from all sin be free.
In Thessalonians we are taught the Lord will come from
heaven,
In Timothy and Titus a shepherd's rule is given.
Philemon marks a brother's love as only brethren know;
Hebrews reveals Christ's priestly works prefigured long
ago.
James teaches without holiness, faith is but vain and dead;
While Peter points the narrow way in which the saints are
led.
John in his three epistles on love delights to dwell;
But Jude gives warning terrible of those once who fell.
The Revelation prophesies that tremendous day
When all the kingdoms of the earth with noise shall pass
away.
'Even so, come, Lord Jesus.'

Author unknown

PRECISE DATING

Archbishop Ussher

Archbishop James Ussher concluded that the world was completed by God on Saturday, 9 October 4004 BC and that the first day of Creation was Sunday, 2 October 4004 BC. He also calculated that Adam and Eve were cast out of the Garden on Monday 10 November 4004 BC. According to his reckoning, the ark came to rest in the mountains of Ararat on Wednesday 5 May 1491 BC. We should not be too doubtful of Bishop Ussher as he was a very learned man and he undertook this task with the greatest gravity. His dates are not far off from the dating of present-day archaeologists.

Here are Bishop Ussher's own words on how he arrived at his conclusion:

For as much as our Christian epoch falls many ages after the beginning of the world, and the number of years before that backward is not only more troublesome, but (unless greater care be taken) more lyable to errour; also it hath pleased our modern chronologers, to adde to that generally received hypothesis (which asserted the Julian years, with their three cycles by a certain mathematical prolepsis, to have run down to the very beginning of the world) an artificial epoch, framed out of three cycles multiplied in themselves; for the Solar Cicle being multiplied by the Lunar, or the number of 28 by 19, produces the great Paschal Cycle of 532 years, and that again multiplied by fifteen, the number of the indiction, there arises the period of 7980 years, which was first (if I mistake not) observed by Robert Lotharing, Bishop of Hereford, in our island of Britain, and 500 years after by Joseph Scaliger fitted for chronological uses, and called by the name of the Julian Period, because it conteined a cycle of so many Julian years. Now if the series of the three minor cicles be from this present year extended backward unto precedent times, the 4713 years before the beginning of our Christian account will be found to be that year into which the first year of the indiction, the first of the Lunar Cicle, and the first of the Solar will fall. Having placed there fore the heads of this period in the kalends of January in that proleptick year, the first of our Christian vulgar account must be reckoned the 4714 of the Julian Period, which, being divided by 15. 19. 28. will present us with the 4 Roman indiction, the 2 Lunar Cycle, and the 10 Solar, which are the principal characters of that year.

We find moreover that the year of our fore-fathers, and the years of the ancient Egyptians and Hebrews were of the same quantity with the Julian, consisting of twelve equal moneths, every of them conteining 30 days, (for it cannot be proved that the Hebrews did use lunary moneths before the Babylonian Captivity) adjoying to the end of the twelfth moneth, the addition of five dayes, and every four year six. And I have observed by the continued succession of these years, as they are delivered in holy writ, that the end of the great Nebuchadnezars and the beginning of Evilmerodachs (his sons) reign, fell out in the 3442 year of the world, but by collation of Chaldean history and the astronomical cannon, it fell out in the 186 year c Nabonasar, and, as by certain connexion, it must follow in the 562 year before the Christian account, and of the Julian Period, the 4152. and from thence I gathered the creation of the world did fall out upon the 710 year of the Julian Period, by placing its beginning in autumn: but for as much as the first day of the world began with the evening of the first day of the week, I have observed that the Sunday, which in the year 710 aforesaid came nearest the Autumnal Equinox, by astronomical tables (notwithstanding the stay of the sun in the dayes of Joshua, and the going back of it in the dayes c Ezekiah) happened upon the 23 day of the Julian October; from thence concluded that from the evening preceding that first day of the Julian year, both the first day of the creation and the first motion of time are to be deduced.

J. Ussher, *The Annals of the World* iv (1658)

Here is a list of dates from *The Annals of the World*:

Creation	4004 BC
Flood	2348 BC
Call of Abraham	1921 BC
Exodus	1491 BC
Foundations of Temple Laid	1012 BC
Destruction of Jerusalem	586 BC
Birth of Christ	4 BC

BIBLES NAMED FROM
TYPOGRAPHICAL ERRORS

The Breeches Bible (1579). So called because Genesis 3.7 was rendered, 'The eyes of them bothe were opened . . . and they sowed figge-tree leaves together, and made themselves breeches.' Printed by Whittingham, Gilby and Sampson.

The Idle Shepherd Bible (1809). So called because 'idol shepherd' is printed as 'the idle shephard' (Zechariah 11.17).

The Bug Bible (1551). So called because Psalm 91.5 is translated, 'Thou shalt not be afraid of bugges by nighte'.

The Placemaker's Bible. So called from a printer's error in Matthew 5.9, 'Blessed are the placemakers [peacemakers], for they shall be called the children of God.'

The Printers' Bible. This text makes David pathetically complain that 'the printers [princes] have persecuted me without a cause' (Psalm 94.16).

The Treacle Bible (1549 – Beck's Bible). 'Is there no tryacle in Gilead?' is printed instead of 'Is there no balm in Gilead?' (Jeremiah 8.22).

The Unrighteous Bible (1652 – Cambridge Press). So called from the printer's error, 'Know ye not that the unrighteous shall inherit the Kingdom of God?' (1 Corinthians 6.9).

The Vinegar Bible (1717). So called because the heading to Luke 20 is given as 'The parable of the Vinegar' (instead of Vineyard). Printed at the Clarendon Press.

The Wicked Bible or *Adulterous Bible* (1632). So called because the word *not* is omitted in the seventh commandment, making it, 'Thou shalt commit adultery.' Printed by Barker and Lucas.

The Denial Bible (1792). The name Philip is substituted for Peter as the apostle who would deny Jesus (Luke 22.34).

The Discharge Bible (1806). Contains the text 'I discharge thee . . . that thou observe these things', instead of 'I charge thee' (1 Timothy 5.21).

The Ears to Ear Bible (1810). 'Who hath ears to ear, let him hear' (Matthew 13.43).

The Fool Bible (1763). Contains the text 'the fool hath said in his heart there is a God' [instead of no God] (Psalm 14.1). The printers where fined 3,000 pounds and all copies were supressed.

The Large Family Bible (1820). Contains the text 'Shall I bring to birth and not cease to bring forth?' for 'for cause to bring forth' (Isaiah 66.9).

The Lions Bible (1804). Contains the text 'The murderer shall surely be put together' instead of 'to death' (Numbers 25.18) And 'but thy son that shall come forth out of thy lions' instead of 'out of thy loins' (Kings 8.19).

The More Sea Bible (1641). Contains the text 'the first heaven and the first earth were passed away and there was more sea' instead of 'there was no more sea' (Revelation 21.1).

The Murderers Bible (1801) Contains the text 'These are murderers, complainers', instead of 'murmurers' (Jude 16).

The Rebekah's Camels Bible (1823). Contains the text 'Rebekah arose, and her camels', instead of 'her damsels' (Genesis 24.61).

The Sin On Bible (1716). Contains the text 'Go and sin on more' instead of 'sin no more' (John 5.14).

The Standing Fishes Bible (1806). Contains the text 'And it shall come to pass that the fishes shall stand on it' instead of 'fishers' (Ezekiel 47.10).

The Sting Bible (1746). Contains the text 'straightway his ears were opened, and the sting of his tongue was loosed, and he spake plain' instead of 'and the string of his tongue was loosed' (Mark 7.35).

The To Remain Bible (1805). Contains the text 'he that was born after the flesh persecuted him that was born after the spirit to remain, even so it is now' (Galatians 4.29) A proofreader queried a comma after 'the spirit' and the editor pencilled in 'to remain'.

The Wife-hater Bible (1810). Contains the text 'If any man come to me, and hates not his father . . . and his own wife also', instead of 'his own life' (Luke 14.26).

Cleansed Outside Bible (1534). In Matthew 23.26, William Tyndale's New Testament reads: 'Thou blind Pharisee, cleanse first, the outside of the cup and platter, that the inside of them may be clean also.' (Tyndale calls attention in 'W. T. To the Reader' that the printer had inverted 'outside' and 'inside'.)

Wife-beater Bible (1551). An edition of the Taverner's Bible contains a marginal note at 1 Peter 3.7 which states 'And if she be not obediente and healpful unto hym, endevoureth to beate the fere of God into her heade, that thereby she may be compelled to learne her dutye and do it.'

Jesus Church Bible (1598). A Geneva Bible reads in 1 John 5.20. 'in his son Jesus Church' instead of 'Jesus Christ'.

Third River Bible (1605). A Geneva Bible at Genesis 2.13 reads 'the third river is Gihon' instead of 'the second river'.

Judas Bible (1608). A Geneva Bible reads. 'Then said Judas' instead of 'Jesus' in John 6.67.

Rosin Bible (1609). A copy of the Douay Version reads as follows in Jeremiah 8.22: 'Is there no rosin in Galaad?' instead of 'no balm'.

He Bible (1611). The first issue of the first edition of the King James Version reads, 'and he went into the city' (Ruth 3.15). It should be 'she went into the city'.

Basketball Bible (1611). In Exodus 38.11, the King James Version Bible says, 'the hoopes of the pillars' instead of 'hookes'.

Pilate's Tile Bible (1612). A KJV at John 19.19 reads, 'And Pilate wrote a tile' instead of 'title'.

Praise Bible (1613). In 1 Corinthians 11.17, this Bible reads, 'I praise you' instead of 'I praise you not'.

No Blame Bible (1632). This KJV Bible says, 'Is there no blame in Gilead' instead of 'no balme' at Jeremiah 8.22.

Religious Bible (1637). In a KJV Bible, at Jeremiah 4.17, it reads 'she hath been religious against me' instead of 'rebellious'.

Forgotten Sins Bible (1638). This KJV Bible reads, 'Her sins which were many are forgotten' as a misprint for 'forgiven' at Luke 7.47.

Vexing Wives Bible (1638). In a KJV Bible at Numbers 25.18 it reads 'for they vex you with their wives' instead of 'with their wiles.'

Subtle Servant Bible (1640). In Genesis 3.1 this KJV Bible reads 'Now the servant was more subtil' instead of 'the serpent'.

Flesh Killer Bible (1648). This KJV reads, 'slew their flesh' instead of 'fish' at Psalm 105.29.

No Miracle Bible (1658). A KJV Bible reads, 'will he do no miracles' (John 7.31) instead of 'do more miracles'.

Cannibals Bible (1682). In Deuteronomy 24.3, a KJV Bible reads 'if the latter husband ate her' instead of 'hate her'.

Not Servants Bible (1698). A KJV reads in Romans 6.17, 'ye were not the servants of sin' instead of 'were the servants'.

Profit Bible (1711). An Oxford KJV edition reads, 'I will declare thy righteousness, and thy works: for they shall profit thee', instead of 'not profit thee' (Isaiah 57.12).

Avenging Obedience Bible (1745). In William Whiston's translation, at 2 Corinthians 10.6 it reads, 'And having readiness to avenge all obedience, when your obedience is fulfilled'. The first 'obedience' should be 'disobedience'.

Child-killer Bible (1795). Mark 7.27 reads in the King James Version 'Let the children first be killed' instead of 'be filled'.

Owl Husband Bible (1944). In a KJV at 1 Peter 3.5, a broken portion of the type face on the word 'own' caused it to appear as 'owl', reading 'being in subjection to their owl husbands'.

Pay for Peace Bible (1966). The first edition of The Jerusalem Bible contained, at Psalm 122.6, the reading 'pay for peace' instead of 'pray for peace'.

Darkness Bible (1970). A New Testament edition of the King James II, by Jay P. Green, contains an erroneous reading at John 1.5: 'and the darkness overcomes it' instead of 'does not overcome it'.

Ship Sale Bible (1987). This edition of The Everyday Bible: New Century Version has Job 3.20 reading, 'Why is it given to those who who are so unhappy?' Normally, computer spell-checkers catch double usages, but this one didn't. It also says in 1 Kings 22.48. 'King Jehoshaphat built trading ships to sale to Ophir for gold' instead of 'sail'.

Unrepentant Ninevites Bible (1989). Heinz Cassierer's God's New Covenant reads in Luke 11.32, 'For when Jonah preached to them, they were not led to repentance', in place of 'were led to repentance'.

Sat On Bible (1993). The NKJV Greek–English Interlinear New Testament, using the Majority text of Zane Hodges and Arthur Farstad (1982), contains a mistranslation in Matthew 21.7, where the Greek text reads 'he sat on them', rather than 'they set [him] on them' (Nashville: Thomas Nelson, 1993).

BIBLES NAMED FROM
PROPER NAMES

Bishop's Bible (1568). The revised edition of Archbishop Parker's version.

Coverdale's Bible (1535). Translated by Miles Coverdale, afterwards Bishop of Exeter. This was the first Bible sanctioned by royal authority.

Cranmer's Bible (1539). This is Coverdale's Bible corrected by Archbishop Cranmer. It was printed in 1540, and in 1549 every parish church was enjoined to have a copy under threat of a penalty of 40s. a month.

The Douay Bible (1581). A translation made by the professors of the Douay College for the use of English boys destined for the Catholic priesthood.

The Geneva Bible. The Bible translated by the English exiles at Geneva. The same as the 'Breeches Bible'.

King James Bible (1611). The Authorized Version; so called because it was undertaken by command of James I.

Matthew Parker's Bible (1539–41). Also known as 'The Great Bible', published in the reign of Henry VIII under the care of Archbishop Parker and his staff. In 1572 several prolegomena were added.

Matthews' Bible (1537). This is Tindal's version. It was so called by John Rogers, superintendent of the English churches in Germany, and was published with notes under the fictitious name of Thomas Matthews.

The Mazarine Bible. The earliest book printed in movable metal type. Called the Mazarine Bible from the *Bibliothèque Mazarine,* founded in Paris by Cardinal Mazarine in 1648.

Sacy's Bible. So called from Isaac Louis Sacy (*Le-maistre*), director of the Port Royal Monastery. He was imprisoned for three years in the Bastille for his Jansenist opinions, and translated the Bible during his captivity (1666–70).

Tyndale's Bible. William Tyndale, or Tindal, having embraced the Reformed religion, retired to Antwerp, where he printed an English translation of the Scriptures. All the copies were bought up, whereupon Tyndale printed a revised edition. The book excited the rancour of the Catholics, who strangled the 'heretic' and burnt his body near Antwerp in 1536.

Wyclif's Bible (1380). First printed in 1850 under this title.

BIBLICAL FILMS

Abraham (1994, TV)
AD (1985 miniseries)
Barabbas (1961)
Ben Hur (versions in 1907, 1925 and 1959)
The Bible (1966)
The Big Fisherman (1959)
The Chosen Prince (1917)
David (1997, TV)
David and Bathsheba (1951)
Demetrius and the Gladiators (1954 sequel to The Robe)
Esther and the King (1960)
The Greatest Story Ever Told (1965)
In the Beginning (2000 miniseries)
Jacob (1994, TV)
Jesus (1979)
Jesus (1999, TV)
Jesus of Nazareth (1977 miniseries)
Joseph and the Amazing Technicolor Dreamcoat (1999, video)
Joseph, King of Dreams (2000 animated video)
Joseph in the Land of Egypt (1914)
King David (1985)
King of Kings (versions in 1927 and 1961)

The Last Temptation of Christ (1988)
The Life of Brian (1979)
Lot in Sodom (1933)
Moses the Lawgiver (1975, TV)
The Nativity (1978, TV)
Noah's Ark (versions in 1929 and 1999, TV)
The Passion of the Christ (2004)
Peter and Paul (1981, TV)
The Prince of Egypt (1998)
Quo Vadis? (1951)
The Robe (1953)
Samson and Delilah (versions in 1949 and 1996, TV)
Sodom and Gomorrah (1962)
Solomon and Sheba (1959)
The Ten Commandments (1923 and 1956)
Veggie Tales (video series)

PROMINENT 3.16s IN THE BIBLE

The most popular verse in the Bible is John 3.16: 'For God so loved the world, that he gave his only begotten Son, that whosoever believeth in him should not perish, but have everlasting life.' Curiously, many of the Bible's 3.16s contain significant guidance and doctrine, as shown below:

Book	3.16	Comment
Genesis	To the woman he said, 'I will greatly increase your pains in childbearing; with pain you will give birth to children. Your desire will be for your husband, and he will rule over you.'	Judgement on mankind

Exodus	Go, assemble the elders of Israel and say to them, 'The LORD, the God of your fathers – the God of Abraham, Isaac and Jacob – appeared to me and said: I have watched over you and have seen what has been done to you in Egypt.	Assurance to Israel
Job	Or why was I not hidden in the ground like a stillborn child, like an infant who never saw the light of day?	Lamentations of Job
Ecclesiastes	And I saw something else under the sun: In the place of judgement –wickedness was there, in the place of justice – wickedness was there.	Unfairness of life
Jeremiah	'In those days, when your numbers have increased greatly in the land,' declares the LORD, 'men will no longer say, "The ark of the covenant of the LORD". It will never enter their minds or be remembered; it will not be missed, nor will another one be made.'	Promise of restoration

Joel	The LORD will roar from Zion and thunder from Jerusalem; the earth and the sky will tremble. But the LORD will be a refuge for his people, a stronghold for the people of Israel.	Assurance
Habakkuk	I heard and my heart pounded, my lips quivered at the sound; decay crept into my bones, and my legs trembled. Yet I will wait patiently for the day of calamity to come on the nation invading us.	Judgement on Israel
Zephaniah	On that day they will say to Jerusalem, 'Do not fear, O Zion; do not let your hands hang limp.'	Reassurance to Israel
Malachi	Then those who feared the LORD talked with each other, and the LORD listened and heard. A scroll of remembrance was written in his presence concerning those who feared the LORD and honoured his name.	God's blessing on his people

Matthew	As soon as Jesus was baptized, he went up out of the water. At that moment heaven was opened, and he saw the Spirit of God descending like a dove and lighting on him.	Jesus' baptism
Luke	John answered, saying to all, 'I indeed baptize you with water; but one mightier than I is coming, whose sandal strap I am not worthy to loose. He will baptize you with the Holy Spirit and fire.'	Promise of the Saviour
Acts	By faith in the name of Jesus, this man whom you see and know was made strong. It is Jesus' name and the faith that comes through him that has given this complete healing to him, as you can all see.	Miraculous healing
1 Corinthians	Do you not know that you are the temple of God and that the Spirit of God dwells in you?	Presence of the Holy Spirit
2 Corinthians	But whenever anyone turns to the Lord, the veil is taken away.	Revelation from the Lord

Galatians	The promises were spoken to Abraham and to his seed. The Scripture does not say 'and to seeds', meaning many people, but 'and to your seed', meaning one person, who is Christ.	Promises to Abraham
Ephesians	I pray that out of his glorious riches he may strengthen you with power through his Spirit in your inner being.	Paul's prayer for believers
Philippians	Only let us live up to what we have already attained.	Exhortation
Colossians	Let the word of Christ dwell in you richly in all wisdom; teaching and admonishing one another in psalms and hymns and spiritual songs, singing with grace in your hearts to the Lord.	Encouragement
2 Thessalonians	Now may the Lord of peace himself give you peace at all times and in every way. The Lord be with all of you.	Assurance

1 Timothy	Beyond all question, the mystery of godliness is great: He appeared in a body, was vindicated by the Spirit, was seen by angels, was preached among the nations, was believed on in the world, was taken up in glory	Summary of Christ's life and eternality
2 Timothy	All Scripture is given by inspiration of God, and is profitable for doctrine, for reproof, for correction, for instruction in righteousness	Origin and value of God's word
James	For where you have envy and selfish ambition, there you find disorder and every evil practice.	Warning against selfishness
1 John	This is how we know what love is: Jesus Christ laid down his life for us. And we ought to lay down our lives for our brothers.	Encouragement to follow after Christ
Revelation	So, because you are lukewarm – neither hot nor cold – I am about to spit you out of my mouth.	Judgement

BIBLE TRANSLATIONS – WORD FOR WORD v THOUGHT FOR THOUGHT

With so many bibles available today, choosing the right one for you can be quite a challenge. One way to choose is to distinguish between those versions that seek to convey word for word accuracy with those that express the main force of the passage. The chart below shows the spectrum of Bibles available on the market today. The more literal are 'word for word' translations while the 'thought for thought' convey the sense not just of the word but the passage of Scripture. In general, 'thought for thought' versions are easier to read but the 'word for word' translations are more accurate.

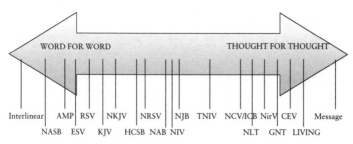

Key:
AMP   Amplified Version
CEV   Contemporary English Version
ESV   English Standard Version
GNT   Good News Translation
HCSB   Holman Christian Standard Bible
KJV   King James Version
NAB   New American Bible
NASB   New American Standard Bible
NCV/ICB   New Century Version
NIV   New International Version
NIrV   New International Readers Version
NJB   New Jerusalem Bible
NKJV   New King James Version
NLT   New Living Translation
NRSV   New Revised Standard Version
RSV   Revised Standard Version
TNIV   Today's New International Version

PARTY OF BIBLE-ABIDING CHRISTIANS

The Party of Bible-Abiding Christians (Partei Bibeltreuer Christen) is a German conservative Christian Fundamental political party. It was founded in 1989. Partei Bibeltreuer Christen is against homosexual marriage, abortion and the separation between state and union. It supports a reference to God in the European Constitution and it strongly supports Israel. Most members are from Baden-Wurttemberg and Saxony.

Further information: www.pbc.de

BIBLICAL FIGURES OF SPEECH

The Bible is a rich source of phrases and idioms and many such words are in our language today, including:

Horse of a different colour – Zechariah 6.2	By the skin of your teeth – Job 19.20
A drop in the bucket – Isaiah 40.15	Feet of clay – Daniel 2.33
Etched in stone – Exodus 31.18	Multitude of sins – 1 Peter 4.8
Suffer fools gladly – 2 Corinthians 11.19	The powers that be – Romans 13.11
Caught 'red-handed' – John 8.4	Still water runs deep – Psalm 23.2
Woe is me! – Job 10.15; Isaiah 6.5	If the shoe fits – Ephesians 6.15

Fox in the henhouse – Luke 13.32	Money where your mouth is – Matthew 17.27
Get your feet wet – Joshua 3.15	Train of thought – Isaiah 6.1
Raising the roof – Mark 2.4	Beating about the bush – Exodus 3.3
Three score and ten – Psalm 90.10	Seeing 'eye to eye' – Isaiah 52.8
Bone of contention – Exodus 12.46	Thorn in the flesh – 2 Corinthians 12.7
Fat's in the fire! – Exodus 29.13	Burning your bridges – 1 Kings 19.21
Made the cut – Romans 2.29	Tough row to hoe – Acts 9.5
Fly in the ointment – Ecclesiastes 10.1	Made a 'scapegoat' – Leviticus 16.10
Mountains from molehills – Matthew 21.21	Stewing in own juices – Deuteronomy 14.21
Handwriting on the wall – Daniel 5.5	Swallow a camel, gag at gnat! – Mathew 23.24
Holier than thou – Isaiah 65.5	All things must pass – Matthew 24.6–8
All things to all men – 1 Corinthians 9.22	Am I my brother's keeper? – Genesis 4.9
An eye for an eye – Exodus 21.24	A tooth for a tooth – Exodus 21.24

At his wits' end – Psalm 107.27	As old as the hills – Job 15.7
Bite the dust – Genesis 3.14	Born again – John 3.3
Faith to move mountains – 1 Corinthians 13.2	Coat of many colours – Genesis 37.3
Eat, drink and be merry – Ecclesiastes 8.15	Fall from grace – Galatians 5.4
Fight the good fight – 1 Timothy 6.12	From strength to strength – Psalm 84.7
How are the mighty fallen – 2 Samuel 1.19	Lamb to the slaughter – Isaiah 53.7
Let there be light – Genesis 1.3	Love thy neighbour – Leviticus 19.18
No rest for the wicked – Isaiah 57.21	O ye of little faith – Matthew 8.26
Sour grapes – Jeremiah 31.29	Apple of his eye – Zechariah 2.8
Blind leading the blind – Matthew 15.14	Bread of life – John 6.35
Cast the first stone – John 8.7	My cup runneth over – Psalm 23.5

BIBLE IMAGERY

GOD	
Consuming fire – Deuteronomy 4.24	Rock – Psalm 18.2, 31
Fountain of water – Jeremiah 2.13	Spirit – John 4.24
Potter, Father – Isaiah 64.8	Husband – Isaiah 54.5
Jealous – Exodus 34.14	Fortress, Tower – Psalm 18.2
'I AM' – Exodus 3.14	Love – 1 John 4.16
Husbandman – Isaiah 54.4–5	Light – 1 John 1.5

JESUS	
Vine of – John 15	Rock – 1 Corinthians 10.4
Door of – John 10.9	Seed – 1 Peter 1.23
Bread of – John 6	Lamb – John 1.29
Light of the World – John 8.12	Lion – Revelation 5.5
Word of God – Revelation 19.13	Author of our faith – Hebrew 12.2
Tree of Life – Genesis 3.22	Head – 1 Corinthians 11.3

HOLY SPIRIT	
Holy Ghost – 2 Peter 1.21	Teacher – John 14.26
Comforter – John 16.7	Dove – Mark 1.10
Spirit of Truth – John 16.13	Rushing wind – Acts 2.2

SCRIPTURE	
Corn – Psalm 78.24	Spirit – John 6.63
Honey – Psalm 19.10, 81.16	Oil – Job 29.6
Milk – Isaiah 28.9; 1 Corinthians 3.2	Word – Psalm 107.20
Wheat – Psalm 147.14	Water – Ephesians 5.26

CHRISTIANS	
Salt and light – Matthew 5.13, 14	Lively stones – 1 Peter 2.5
Priests – Revelation 5.10	Vessels – 2 Corinthians 4.7
Sheep – Psalm 100.3	Epistles – 2 Corinthians 3.2
Clay – Isaiah 64.8	Virgins – 2 Corinthians 11.2
Temples – 2 Corinthians 6.16	Sons – 1 John 3.2
Seeds – Romans 9.8; Genesis 4.25	Houses – Hebrews 3.6
Trees – Isaiah 61.3	

JESUS CHRIST IN EVERY BOOK OF THE BIBLE

From Genesis to Revelation, the Bible has a golden thread running through it that weaves the promise, power and passion of the Messiah.

Old Testament	Messiah Picture
Genesis 3.24	Tree of Life
Exodus 3.14	I AM
Leviticus 23.12	Sacrificial Lamb
Numbers 11.6	Manna
Deuteronomy 30.19	Life
Joshua 2.18	Scarlet cord
Judges 7.20	Sword of the Lord
Ruth 4.14	Redeemer
1 Samuel 12.12	King
2 Samuel 3.1	House of David
1 Kings 6.12	Solomon's Temple
2 Kings 4.41	Antidote
1 Chronicles 17.11	Promised Messiah
2 Chronicles 8.16	The finished Temple
Ezra 1.2	Cyrus, King of Persia
Nehemiah 8.15	Shelter

Esther 4.11	Golden Sceptre
Job 9.33	Umpire
Psalm 110.4	Melchizedek
Proverbs 4.7	Wisdom
Ecclesiastes 7.11	Wisdom
Song of Solomon 2.1	Rose of Sharon
Isaiah 9.6	Prince of Peace
Jeremiah 2.13	Living Water
Lamentations 3.1	Man of Sorrows
Ezekiel 1.10	Son of Man
Daniel 3.45	Fourth Man
Hosea 2.16–20	Bridegroom
Joel 2.32	Salvation
Amos 9.9	Sifter
Obadiah 1.17	Mount Zion
Jonah 1.17	Rescuer
Micah 4.10	Redeemer
Nahum 1.7	Refuge
Habakkuk 2.4	Faith
Zephaniah 3.9	Purifier
Haggai 2.7	Desire of nation
Zechariah 9.9	Salvation King
Malachi 2.7	Messenger

New Testament	Messiah Picture
Matthew 1.1	Son of David
Mark 1.11	Son of God
Luke 5.24	Son of Man
John 1.14	Word of God
Acts 9.3	Shining Light
Romans 5.8	Substitute
1 Corinthians 1.18	Power of God
2 Corinthians 11.2	Husband
Galatians 5.1	Deliverer
Ephesians 2.20	Cornerstone
Philippians 2.10	Lord
Colossians 1.27	The hope of glory
1 Thessalonians 1.10	Rescuer
2 Thessalonians 1.8	Judge
1 Timothy 1.15	Saviour
2 Timothy 1.10	Saviour
Titus 2.11	Grace of God
Philemon 1.16	Brother
Hebrews 3.1	High priest
James 1.5	Wisdom
1 Peter 2.24	Healer
2 Peter 2.20	Saviour

1 John 1.1	Word of Life
2 John 1.3	Father's Son
3 John 1.1	The Truth
Jude 1.14	Enoch
Revelation 17.14	Lord of Lords

THE COMPLUTENSIAN POLYGLOT BIBLE

In 1502, Cardinal Fransisco Ximenez de Cisneros (Archbishop of Toledo in Spain, Primas of Spain and Grand Inquisitor) had the idea of producing a Bible in Hebrew, Greek, Aramaic and Latin. This became known as the Complutensian – from the Latin name (Complutum) of the Spanish city Alcala, where the scholars met – Polyglot (many languages) Bible.

The Complutensian Polyglot Bible was published as a six-volume set, some time after its completion in 1517. Today, there are fewer than 130 copies surviving. The Old Testament is contained in the first four volumes and each page consists of three parallel columns of Hebrew (outside), Latin Vulgate (middle) and Greek Septuagint (inside). The Pentateuch also has Aramaic and another Latin translation.

The New Testament forms the fifth and sixth volumes and contains Hebrew, Aramaic and Greek dictionaries, vocabulary lists and a brief Hebrew grammar.

Before the Polyglot Bible was completed, news of the project reached the Dutch theologian Desiderius Erasmus who published his rushed edition of the Greek New Testament that became known as the Textus Receptus (Received Text) and formed the foundation of the King James Version published in 1611. Because Erasmus had the patronage of Pope Leo X, publication of the Polyglot Bible was delayed until 1520, while

Erasmus' edition was published in 1516. It was not widely distributed until 1522.

Five months after the completion of the Complutensian Polyglot Bible, Cardinal Jimenez died. He never saw its publication.

NAMES AND OFFICES OF JESUS CHRIST

Advocate (1 John 2.1)
Almighty (Revelation 1.8; Matthew 28.18)
Alpha and Omega (Revelation 1.8, 22.13)
Amen (Revelation 3.14)
Apostle of our Profession (Hebrews 3.1)
Atoning Sacrifice for our Sins (1 John 2.2)
Author of Life (Acts 3.15)
Author and Perfecter of our Faith (Hebrews 12.2)
Author of Salvation (Hebrews 2.10)
Beginning and End (Revelation 22.13)
Blessed and only Ruler (1 Timothy 6.15)
Bread of God (John 6.33)
Bread of Life (John 6.35, 48)
Capstone (Acts 4.11; 1 Peter 2.7)
Chief Cornerstone (Ephesians 2.20)
Chief Shepherd (1 Peter 5.4)
Christ (1 John 2.22)
Creator (John 1.3)
Deliverer (Romans 11.26)
Door (John 10.9)
Eternal Life (1 John 1.2, 5.20)
Everlasting Father (Isaiah 9.6)
Faithful and True Witness (Revelation 3.14)
Faithful and True (Revelation 19.11)
Faithful Witness (Revelation 1.5)

[49]

First and Last (Revelation 1.17; 2.8; 22.13)
Firstborn from the Dead (Revelation 1.5)
God (John 1.1, 20.28; Romans 9.5; Hebrews 1.8;
2 Peter 1.1; 1 John 5.20)
Good Shepherd (John 10.11, 14)
Great Shepherd (Hebrews 13.20)
Great High Priest (Hebrews 4.14)
Head of the Church (Ephesians 1.22, 4.15, 5.23)
Heir of all things (Hebrews 1.2)
High Priest (Hebrews 2.17)
Holy One (Acts 3.14)
Holy and True (Revelation 3.7)
Hope (1 Timothy 1.1)
Hope of Glory (Colossians 1.27)
Horn of Salvation (Luke 1.69)
I Am (John 8.58)
Image of God (2 Corinthians 4.4)
King Eternal (1 Timothy 1.17)
King of Israel (John 1.49)
King of the Jews (Matthew 27.11)
King of Kings (1 Timothy 6.15; Revelation 19.16)
King of the Ages (Revelation 15.3)
Lamb (Revelation 13.8)
Lamb of God (John 1.29)
Lamb Without Blemish (1 Peter 1.19)
Last Adam (1 Corinthians 15.45)
Life (John 14.6; Colossians 3.4)
Light of the World (John 8.12)
Lion of the Tribe of Judah (Revelation 5.5)
Living One (Revelation 1.18)
Living Stone (1 Peter 2.4)
Lord (2 Peter 2.20)
Lord of All (Acts 10.36)
Lord of Glory (1 Corinthians 2.8)
Lord of lords (Revelation 19.16)
LORD [YHWH] our Righteousness (Jeremiah 23.6)

Man from Heaven (1 Corinthians 15.48)
Mediator of the New Covenant (Hebrews 9.15)
Mighty God (Isaiah 9.6)
Morning Star (Revelation 22.16)
Offspring of David (Revelation 22.16)
One Mediator (1 Timothy 2.5)
Only Begotten Son of God (John 1.18; 1 John 4.9)
Our Great God and Savior (Titus 2.13)
Our Holiness (1 Corinthians 1.30)
Our Husband (2 Corinthians 11.2)
Our Protection (2 Thessalonians 3.3)
Our Redemption (1 Corinthians 1.30)
Our Righteousness (1 Corinthians 1.30)
Our Sacrificed Passover Lamb (1 Corinthians 5.7)
Power of God (1 Corinthians 1.24)
Precious Cornerstone (1 Peter 2.6)
Prince of Peace (Isaiah 9.6)
Prophet (Acts 3.22)
Resurrection and Life (John 11.25)
Righteous Branch (Jeremiah 23.5)
Righteous One (Acts 7.52; 1 John 2.1)
Rock (1 Corinthians 10.4)
Root of David (Revelation 5.5, 22.16)
Ruler of God's Creation (Revelation 3.14)
Ruler of the Kings of the Earth (Revelation 1.5)
Saviour (Ephesians 5.23; Titus 1.4, 3.6; 2 Peter 2.20)
Son of David (Luke 18.39)
Son of God (John 1.49; Hebrews 4.14)
Son of Man (Matthew 8.20)
Son of the Most High God (Luke 1.32)
Source of eternal salvation for all who obey him
(Hebrews 5.9)
The stone the builders rejected (Acts 4.11)
True Bread (John 6.32)
True God (1 John 5.20)
True Light (John 1.9)

True Vine (John 15.1)
Truth (John 14.6)
Way (John 14.6)
Wisdom of God (1 Corinthians 1.24)
Wonderful Counsellor (Isaiah 9.6)
Word (John 1.1)
Word of God (Revelation 19.13)

NEW TESTAMENT COINS

Tribute Penny – Tiberius Caesar

Jesus, referring to a 'penny' asked, 'Whose is this image and superscription?' When told it was Caesar, he said, 'Give to Caesar what is Caesar's and to God what is God's' (Matthew 22.20–21). Since Tiberius was Caesar at the time, this denarius type is attributed by scholars as the 'penny' referred to in the Bible. Hoard evidence indicates the straight leg type was minted earlier and thus is more likely to have been in circulation in Jerusalem during Jesus' lifetime.

Judas' 30 Pieces of Silver – Herod the Great

'Then one of the 12, called Judas Iscariot, went unto the chief priests, and said unto them, "What are you willing to give me if I hand him over to you?" And they covenanted with him for 30 pieces of silver' (Matthew 26.14–15). Shekels of Tyre were the only currency accepted at the Jerusalem Temple and are the most likely coinage with which Judas was paid for the betrayal of Christ. The silver shekels and half-shekels of Tyre were minted from *c.* 126 BC until *c.* AD 57.

Temple Tax – Herod the Great

At the Great Temple in Jerusalem the annual tax levied on Jews was one half-shekel per male. The half-shekel and shekel were not always used in everyday commerce, but were the only coins accepted by the Temple. Many taxpayers required a currency exchange, so money changers set up in the Temple court. Jesus found this business and their shouting (advertising rates) offensive, so he threw over their tables.

'. . . go to the lake and throw out your line. Take the first fish that you catch; open its mouth and you will find a coin. Take it and give it to them [the Temple tax collectors] for my tax and yours' (Matthew 17.24–27). Since the tax was one half-shekel per man the coin would have to be a shekel to pay the tax for both Jesus and Peter. Silver shekels and half-shekels of Tyre were minted from *c.* 126 BC until *c.* AD 57. Any coin minted prior to AD 32 may have circulated in Jerusalem during Jesus' lifetime.

The Widow's Mite

> Jesus said, 'I tell you the truth, this poor widow put more into the treasury than all the others. For all of them have contributed out of their wealth; but she out of her poverty, put in everything – all she had to live on.' (Mark 12.43)

These coins are bronze lepton and prutah of Alexander Jannaeus, the Hasmonean King of Judea from 103 to 76 BC. Although these coins were minted long before Christ's lifetime, they were still in circulation during the first century AD. Because leptons and prutahs, were the lowest denomination coins that circulated in Jerusalem during Christ's lifetime, they are believed to be the coins referred to in the biblical story of the poor widow. The lepton is the very smallest denomination and is probably the true 'widow's mite'. In fact, the lepton is probably the lowest denomination coin ever struck by any nation in all of history! Lepton and prutah were carelessly and crudely struck, usually off-centre and on small flans. Because they circulated for a long period, they are usually very worn. Legends are almost always unreadable. The actual size of a prutah is less than half an inch in diameter. A lepton is usually about the same diameter as a pencil eraser.

Ref: http://www.forumancientcoins.com/

GENESIS AND REVELATION COMPARED

Genesis

1. Genesis, the book of the beginning
2. The Earth created (1.1)
3. Satan's first rebellion (3.1)
4. Sun, moon and stars for the Earth's government (1.14–16)
5. Sun to govern the day (1.16)
6. Darkness called night (1.5)
7. Waters called seas (1.10)
8. A river for Earth's blessing (2.10–14)
9. Man in God's image (1.26)
10. Entrance of sin (3)
11. Curse pronounced (3.14, 17)
12. Death entered (3.19)
13. Cherubim, first mentioned in connection with man (3.24)
14. Man driven out from Eden (3.24)
15. Tree of life guarded (3.24)
16. Sorrow and suffering enter (3.17–19)

Revelation

1. Apocalypse, the book of the end.
2. The Earth passed away (21.1)
3. Satan's final rebellion (20.7–10)
4. Sun, moon, and stars, connected with the Earth's judgement (6.13, 8.12, 16.8)
5. No need of the sun (21.23)
6. 'No night there' (22.5)
7. 'No more sea' (21.1)
8. A river for the New Earth (22.1, 2)
9. Man headed by one in Satan's image (13)
10. End of sin (21)
11. 'No more curse' (22.3)
12. 'No more death' (21.4)
13. Cherubim, finally mentioned in connection with man (4.6)
14. Man restored (22)
15. 'Right to the Tree of Life' (22.14)
16. No more sorrow (21.4)

Genesis	Revelation
17. Man's religion, art, and science, resorted to for enjoyment, apart from God (4.19–22)	17. Man's religion, luxury, art, and science, in their full glory, judged and destroyed by God (18)
18. Nimrod, a great rebel and king, and hidden anti-God, the founder of Babylon (10.8, 9)	18. The Beast, the great rebel, a king, and manfiested anti-God, the reviver of Babylon (13—17)
19. A flood from God to destroy an evil generation (6.17)	19. A flood from Satan to destroy an elect generation (12)
20. The Rainbow, the token of God's covenant with the Earth (9.13)	20. The Rainbow, denoting God's remembrance of his covenant with the Earth (4.3; 10.1)
21. Sodom and Egypt, the place of corruption and temptation (13.19)	21. Sodom and Egypt again (spiritually representing Jerusalem) (11.8)
22. A confederacy against Abraham's people overthrown (14.13–16)	22. A confederacy against Abraham's seed overthrown (12)
23. Marriage of the first Adam (2.18–23)	23. Marriage of last Adam (19.6–9)
24. A bride sought for Abraham's son (Isaac) and found (24)	24. A Bride made ready and brought to Abraham's Son (19.9) See Matthew 1.1
25. Two angels acting for God on behalf of his people (19.1–29)	25. Two witnesses acting for God on behalf of his people (11.1–14)
26. A promised seed to possess the gate of his enemies (22.17)	26. The promised seed coming into possession (11.18)
27. Man's dominion ceased and Satan's begun (3.24)	27. Satan's dominion ended, and man's restored (22)

Genesis	Revelation
28. The old serpent causing sin, suffering and death (3.1)	28. The old serpent bound for 1,000 years (20.1–3)
29. The doom of the old serpent pronounced (3.15)	29. The doom on the old serpent executed (20.10)
30. Sun, moon and stars, associated with Israel (37.9)	30. Sun, moon and stars, associated again with Israel (12.1)

PROPHECIES FULFILLED BY JESUS CHRIST

The Bible has many detailed prophecies that have been fulfilled with amazing accuracy. Here is a list of the fifty major messianic prophecies fulfilled through the life, ministry, death and resurrection of Jesus:

	Prophetic Scripture	Prophecy	Fulfilled
1	Genesis 3.15	seed of a woman	Galatians 4.4
2	Genesis 12.3; Genesis 22.18	descendant of Abraham	Matthew 1.1; Acts 3.25
3	Genesis 17.19; Genesis 21.12	descendant of Isaac	Luke 3.34
4	Genesis 28.14; Numbers 24.17	descendant of Jacob	Matthew 1.2; Luke 3.23–34
5	Genesis 49.10	from the tribe of Judah	Luke 3.23–33

	Prophetic Scripture	Prophecy	Fulfilled
6	Isaiah 9.6; 11.1–5; Jeremiah 23.5–6	descendant of David	Matthew 1.1; Luke 3.23–31
7	Isaiah 11.1	descendant of Jesse	Luke 3.23, 32
8	Ezekiel 37.24 Micah 5.2	will shepherd his people	Matthew 2.6
9	Isaiah 9.7	heir to the throne of David	Luke 1.32–33
10	Micah 5.2	his pre-existence	Colossians 1.17
11	Isaiah 9.6; Micah 5.2	eternal existence	John 8.58; 11; 14; Colossians 1.15–19
12	Psalm 45.6–7; Psalm 102.25–27	anointed and eternal	Hebrews 1.8–12
13	Psalm 110.1	called Lord	Matthew 22.43–45
14	Isaiah 33.22	judge	John 5.30
15	Psalms 2.6	king	Matthew 27.37
16	Micah 5.2	born in Bethlehem	Matthew 2.1; Luke 2.4
17	Isaiah 7.14	to be born of a virgin	Matthew 1.18; Luke 1.26–27, 30–31

	Prophetic Scripture	Prophecy	Fulfilled
18	Psalm 72.9	worshipped by shepherds	Luke 2.8–15
19	Psalm 72.10	honoured by kings	Matthew 2.1–11
20	Jeremiah 31.15	slaughter of children	Matthew 2.16–18
21	Hosea 11.1	flight to Egypt	Matthew 2.14–15
22	Isaiah 40.3–5	the way prepared	Matthew 3.1, 2; Luke 3.3–6
23	Malachi 3.1	preceded by a forerunner	Luke 7.24, 27
24	Malachi 4.5–6	preceded by Elijah	Matthew 11.13–14
25	Psalm 2.7; Proverbs 30.4	declared the Son of God	Matthew 3.17; Luke 1.32
26	Isaiah 9.5–6; Jeremiah 23.5–6	God's name applied to him	Romans 10.9; Philippians 2.9–11
27	Isaiah 11.2; 61.1; Psalm 45.8	anointing of Holy Spirit	Matthew 3.16, 17; John 3.34; Acts 10.38
28	Isaiah 9.1–2	Galilean ministry	Matthew 4.13–16
29	Psalm 78.2–4	speaks in parables	Matthew 13.34–35

	Prophetic Scripture	Prophecy	Fulfilled
30	Isaiah 56.7; Jeremiah 7.11	Temple becomes a house of merchandise instead of prayer	Matthew 21.13; John 2.6
31	Psalm 69.9	zeal of Jews for the Temple instead of God	John 2.17
32	Deuteronomy 18.15, 18	a prophet	Matthew 21.11; Acts 3.20; 22
33	Isaiah 29.18; 35.5–6	blind, deaf and lame are healed by the Messiah	Matthew 11.3–5; Luke 7.22
34	Isaiah 40.11; 42.2–3; 53.7	Messiah will be meek and mild	Matthew 11.29, 12.18–20; Hebrews 4.15
35	Isaiah 53.9	Be sinless and without guile	1 Peter 2.22
36	Isaiah 42.1; 49.1	will minister to Gentiles	Matthew 12.18–21; Luke 2.32
37	Isaiah 61.1–2	to bind up the brokenhearted	Luke 4.18–19
38	Isaiah 53.12; 59.16	to intercede for the people	Romans 8.34; Hebrews 7.25
39	Psalms 69.6; 118.22; Isaiah 53.3; 8.14; 28.16; 53.3; 63.3	rejected by his own people, the Jews	Luke 23.18; John 1.11; 7.5; 48; Acts 4.11; 1 Peter 2.6–8

	Prophetic Scripture	Prophecy	Fulfilled
40	Psalm 118.22	rejected by the Jewish leadership	Matthew 21.42; John 7.48
41	Psalm 2.1–2	plotted against by Jews and Gentiles alike	Acts 4.27
42	Psalm 110.4	priest after the order of Melchizedek	Hebrews 5.5–6
43	Zechariah 9.9	enter Jerusalem on donkey	Mark 11.7, 9, 11; Luke 19.35–37
44	Haggai 2.7–9; Malachi 3.1	entered the Temple with authority	Matthew 21.12; Luke 2.27–38
45	Psalm 8.2	adored by infants	Matthew 21.15–16
46	Isaiah 53.1	not believed	John 12.37–38
47	Zechariah 13.7	sheep of the Shepherd scattered	Matthew 26.31; Mark 14.50
48	Psalm 41.9; 55.13–14	betrayed by a close friend	Matthew 10.4; Luke 22.47–48
49	Zechariah 11.12	betrayed for thirty pieces of silver	Matthew 26.14–15
50	Hosea 6.2	resurrected on the third day	Luke 24.6–7

JESUS AND JOSEPH COMPARED

The story of Joseph is especially connected to the narrative of the Saviour because Joseph's life typified the life of Jesus in many ways. There are at least 100 similarities between Joseph and Jesus and that is why Joseph is known as the Messianic Patriarch. This is a partial comparison between Joseph and Jesus:

Category	Joseph	Jesus
Occupation	A shepherd 'feeding the flock' (Genesis 37.2)	Christ is the good shepherd (John 10.11)
Opposition to evil	Joseph brought to his father evil reports of his brothers (Genesis 37.2)	I testify that what it (the world) does is evil (John 7.7)
Father's love	First born of Rachel the beloved wife of Jacob (Genesis 30.22–24)	God the Father gave his son Jesus a special privilege (Proverbs 8.22)
Hatred of his brethren	Jacob's love brought enmity (Genesis 37.4)	Revealed his father's heart and faced man's enmity (John 14.10)
Sent forth by his father	Jacob sent forth Joseph (Genesis 37.12–14)	Son obeyed (Hebrews 10.7)
Seeks the welfare of his brethren	'Go and see if all is well with your brothers' (Genesis 37.14)	Sent with a definite objective – seek his brethren (John 1.11)

Disbelieved	'Here comes that dreamer!' they said to each other. 'Come now, let's kill him and throw him into one of these cisterns and say that a ferocious animal devoured him. Then we'll see what comes of his dreams' (Genesis 37.19–20)	They put a staff in his right hand and knelt in front of him and mocked him. 'Hail, king of the Jews!' they said. (Matthew 27.29)
Insulted	So when Joseph came to his brothers, they stripped him of his robe – the richly ornamented robe he was wearing – and they took him and threw him into the cistern (Genesis 37.23–24)	When the soldiers crucified Jesus, they took his clothes, dividing them into four shares, one for each of them, with the undergarment remaining (Mark 15.24)
Cast into a pit	So when Joseph came to his brothers, they stripped him of his robe – the richly ornamented robe he was wearing– – and they took him and threw him into the cistern (Genesis 37.23)	For as Jonah was three days and three nights in the belly of a huge fish, so the Son of Man will be three days and three nights in the heart of the earth (Matthew 12.40)

Betrayed	'Come, let's sell him to the Ishmaelites and not lay our hands on him; after all, he is our brother, our own flesh and blood.' His brothers agreed (Genesis 37.27)	Look, the hour is near, and the Son of Man is betrayed into the hands of sinners (Matthew 26.45)
Blessings to others	From the time he put him in charge of his household and of all that he owned, the LORD blessed the household of the Egyptian because of Joseph (Genesis 39.5)	And he took the children in his arms, put his hands on them and blessed them (Mark 10.16)
Age	Joseph was thirty years old when he entered the service of Pharaoh king of Egypt (Genesis 41.46)	Now Jesus himself was about thirty years old when he began his ministry (Luke 3.23)

FATHERS AND SONS

The Bible teaches that godliness is not inherited and, although godly conduct is to be desired, it does not guarantee that future generations will automatically follow in the way of their holy parents. To illustrate this, here are some examples of *godly fathers* who had *sinful sons*:

Godly father	Sinful son(s)
Isaac the Promised Son	Esau sold his birthright to his brother Jacob (Genesis 25)
Aaron the Levite	Nadab and Abihu offered 'strange fire' on the altar of incense (Leviticus 10)
Gideon the Judge	Abimelech murdered 70 of his brothers (Judges 9)
Eli the High Priest	Hophni and Phineas were dishonest priests (1 Samuel 2)
Samuel the Kingmaker	Joel and Abijah took bribes and distorted justice (1 Samuel 8)
David the Lord's Chosen	Amnon raped his half-sister (2 Samuel 13)
David the Lord's Chosen	Absalom rebelled against his father (2 Samuel 15)
David the Lord's Chosen	Adonijah tried to usurp Solomon (1 Kings 1)
Solomon the Wise	Rehoboam started a civil war (1 Kings 12)
King Jehoshaphat	Joram murdered six of his brothers (2 Chronicles 21)

Godly father	Sinful son(s)
King Jotham	Ahaz sacrificed his son to idols (2 Kings 16)
King Hezekiah	Manasseh – Judah's most evil king (2 Kings 21)
King Josiah	Jehoiakim did evil in God's sight (Jeremiah 36)

In contrast, the Bible records some *godly sons* who followed their *godless fathers*:

Godly son	Sinful father
Jonathan made a covenant with David	King Saul
King Asa was a godly ruler	King Abijam
King Hezekiah was a godly ruler	King Ahaz
King Josiah was a godly ruler	King Amon

BIBLICAL PLAGUES

God sent plagues (natural disasters, war, famine and disease) upon nations and individuals to show his righteousness judgement and as a warning to urge people to repent. Prominent biblical plagues include:

Nation/ Person	Plague of . . .
Egypt: 10 plagues (Exodus 7–12)	Water turned to blood Frogs Lice Flies (beetles) Cattle disease Boils Hail Locusts Darkness Death of firstborn
Israel: 8 plagues (Deuteronomy 28, 32; Numbers 16.25; 2 Samuel 24)	Death by the sword Death by fire Unnamed plague to eradicate lust Death for unbelief Death by snakes Death for immorality Death for looking into the Ark of God Death due to David's census
Philistia (1 Samuel 5)	Tumours for capturing the Ark of God
Syria (2 Kings 6)	Blindness for attacking Israel

Tribulation Plagues upon all nations (Revelation 6—16)	Conquest (white horse) War (red horse) Famine (black horse) Death (pale horse) Earthquake (sixth seal) Destruction (first trumpet) Oceans turned to blood (second trumpet) Fresh water turned bitter (third trumpet) Sun, moon and stars darkened (fourth trumpet) Scorpion stings upon mankind (fifth trumpet) Third of all people killed (sixth trumpet) Sores upon mankind (first vial) All sea life destroyed (second vial) Rivers turned to blood (third vial) Scorching by sun (fourth vial) Darkness (fifth vial) Euphrates river dries up (sixth vial) Destruction of Babylon (seventh vial)
Moses (Exodus 4)	Leprosy
Miriam (Numbers 12)	Leprosy
Nabal (1 Samuel 25)	Death
Uzziah (2 Chronicles 26)	Leprosy
Gehazi (2 Kings 5)	Leprosy
Herod (Acts 12)	Death

CLARENCE LARKIN: CHARTS

 American Baptist minister Clarence Larkin (1850–1924) found Christ at the age of 19. In 1882, he went directly from being a businessman into the ministry. Through his study of the Scriptures, he began to make large wall charts, which he titled, 'Prophetic Truth', that were widely circulated for use in the pulpit. This led to his being invited to teach in two Bible institutes.

He spent three years of his life designing and drawing the charts and preparing the text. Because it had a large and wide circulation, the first edition was soon exhausted. Larkin followed this masterpiece with other books: *Rightly Dividing the Word, The Book of Daniel, Spirit World, Second Coming of Christ*, and *A Medicine Chest for Christian Practitioners*, a handbook on evangelism.

Larkin, a kind and gentle man, deplored the tendency of writers to say uncharitable things about each other, so he earnestly sought to avoid criticisms and to satisfy himself with simply presenting his understanding of the Scriptures. Though he did not intend to publish his own works, the Lord led in that direction. During the last five years of his life, the demand for Larkin's books made it necessary for him to give up the pastorate and devote his full time to writing.

Further information about Clarence Larkin and his famous charts can be found at www.larkinestate.com

COVENANTS IN THE BIBLE

Covenant: a contract or agreement between two parties
In the Old Testament the Hebrew word *berith* is always thus translated. *Berith* is derived from a root which means 'to cut', and hence a covenant is a 'cutting', with reference to the cutting or dividing of animals into two parts, and the contracting

parties passing between them, in making a covenant (Genesis 15.7–21; Jeremiah 34.18, 19). The corresponding word in the New Testament Greek is *diatheke,* which is, however, rendered 'testament' generally in the Authorized Version. It ought to be rendered, just as the word *berith* of the Old Testament, 'covenant'.

M.G. Easton, *Easton's Bible Dictionary, Illustrated Bible Dictionary*, Third Edition, published by Thomas Nelson, 1897

Covenant	Between	Significance
Edenic Covenant (Genesis 1.26–31; 2.16–17)	God and man	God undertakes to provide for man
Adamic Covenant (Genesis 3.16–19)	God and man	Promise of a redeemer
Noahic Covenant (Genesis 9.1–18)	God and Noah	Principle of human government
Abrahamic Covenant (Genesis 12.1–4; 22.15–18)	God and Abraham	Promises to Abraham and his descendants
Mosaic Covenant (Exodus 19.4–6; 24.1–8	God and Israel	Details God's promises and demands from his chosen people
Deuteronomic Covenant (Deuteronomy 30.1–10)	God and Israel	Blessings and cursings
Davidic Covenant (2 Samuel 7.4–16)	God and the line of David	An everlasting kingdom for the descendants of David
The New Covenant (Jeremiah 31.31–34)	God and his people	Everlasting provision through the promised Messiah

BIBLE BAPTISMS

The book of Acts contains many examples of people being baptized, including:

Three thousand people	Acts 2.41
Simon the sorcerer	Acts 8.12–13
Ethiopian eunuch	Acts 8.38
Saul of Tarsus	Acts 9.18
Cornelius	Acts 10.48
Lydia	Acts 16.14–15
Philippian jailer	Acts 16.33
Crispus the synagogue ruler	Acts 18.8
Twelve men in Ephesus	Acts 19.1–7

SATANIC APPELLATIONS

\Sa"tan\ (n.): *Evil adversary of God and humanity, often identified with the leader of the fallen angels; the Devil.*
Easton's 1897 Bible Dictionary

Accuser of the brethren	Revelation 12.10
Adversary	Job 1.6
Angel of light	2 Corinthians 11.14–15
Apollyon	Revelation 9.11
Beelzebub	Matthew 12.24
Belia	2 Corinthians 6.15
Day Star	Isaiah 14.12
Devil	Hebrews 2.14
Diabolos	Revelation 12.9
Enemy	Matthew 13.39
Father of lies	John 8.44
God of this world	2 Corinthians 4.4
Prince of the power of the air	Ephesians 2.2
Prince of this world	John 12.31

Roaring lion	1 Peter 5.8
Satan	Zechariah 3.1
Spirit that works . . . disobedience	Ephesians 2.:2
Tempter	1 Thessalonians 3.5

LOST BOOKS

These books are referred to in the Bible, but they are not included among the books of the Bible.

Subject	Bible Reference
Book of the Wars of the Lord	Numbers 21.14
Book of Jashar	Joshua 10.13
The Acts of Solomon	1 Kings 11.41
Annals of the Kings of Israel	1 Kings 14.19
Annals of the Kings of Judah	1 Kings 14.29
Book of the Kings of Israel	1 Chronicles 9.1
Records of the Seer Samuel	1 Chronicles 29.29
Records of the Prophet Nathan	1 Chronicles 29.29
Records of the Seer Gad	1 Chronicles 29.29
History of the Prophet Nathan	2 Chronicles 9.29
Prophecy of Ahijah the Shilonite	2 Chronicles 9.29
Visions of the Seer Iddo	2 Chronicles 9.29
Records of the Prophet Shemaiah and the Seer Iddo	2 Chronicles 12.15
Story of the Prophet Iddo	2 Chronicles 13.22
Book of the Kings of Judah and Israel	2 Chronicles 16.11
Annals of Jehu son of Hanani	2 Chronicles 20.34
Commentary on the Book of the Kings	2 Chronicles 24.27
Acts of Uzziah	2 Chronicles 26.22
Book of the Kings of Israel and Judah	2 Chronciles 27.7
Vision of the Prophet Isaiah	2 Chronicles 32.32
Annals of the Kings of Israel	2 Chronicles 33.18
Record of the Seers	2 Chronciles 33.19
Book of the Annals	Nehemiah 12.23

The Bible: A history, the making and impact of the Bible
by Miller and Huber published by Lion

THE TEN COMMANDMENTS
IN RHYME

1 Thou no gods shalt have but me,
2 Before no idol bend the knee.
3 Take not the Lord's name in vain,
4 Neither the Sabbath day profane.
5 Give thy parents their honour due,
6 And ensure no murder thou do.
7 Abstain from words and deeds unclean,
8 Steal not, for by God thou art seen.
9 Tell not a wicked lie, nor love it,
10 What is thy neighbours', do not covet.

THE BIBLE IN FIFTY WORDS

There are over 700,000 words in the King James Bible. This is
the condensed version:

God made
Adam bit
Noah arked
Abraham split
Joseph ruled
Jacob fooled
Bush talked
Moses balked
Pharaoh plagued
People walked
Sea divided
Tablets guided
Promise landed
Saul freaked
David peeked
Prophets warned

Jesus born
God walked
Love talked
Anger crucified
Hope died
Love rose
Spirit flamed
Word spread
God remained.

Anon

THE HOLY SPIRIT – NINE GIFTS AND NINE FRUITS

1 Corinthians 12.7–11

Now to each one the manifestation of the Spirit is given for the *common good*. To one there is given through the Spirit the message of *wisdom*, to another the message of *knowledge* by means of the same Spirit, to another *faith* by the same Spirit, to another gifts of *healing* by that one Spirit, to another *miraculous powers*, to another *prophecy*, to another *distinguishing between spirits*, to another *speaking in different kinds of tongues*, and to still another *the interpretation of tongues*. All these are the work of one and the same Spirit, and he gives them to each one, just as he determines.

Galatians 5.22–23

But the fruit of the Spirit is *love, joy, peace, patience, kindness, goodness, faithfulness, gentleness and self-control*. Against such things there is no law.

THE LORD'S PRAYER IN DIFFERENT LANGUAGES

English

Our Father, which art in heaven
Hallowed be thy Name;
Thy kingdom come;
Thy will be done
In earth as it is in heaven.
Give us this day our daily bread;
And forgive us our trespasses,
As we forgive those who trespass against us.
And lead us not into temptation,
But deliver us from evil:
For thine is the kingdom,
The power and the glory,
For ever and ever.
Amen.

Book of Common Prayer (1549)

Cornish

Agon Taze nye, eze en Neve,
Benegas bo tha Hanow.
Tha Gwlaskath gwrenz doaz;
Tha Voth bo gwreze,
En Noer pecarra en Neve.
Ro tha nye an journama gon bara pub death,
Ha gave tha nye gon pehasow
Pecarra tel era nye gava angye
Neb eze peha war agon bidn.
Ha na raze gon lewa en antall,
Buz gweeth nye thurt droeg.
Rag an Gwlaskath Che a beaw,
Han Nearth, han Worrians,
Rag nevra venitha.
Andelna ra bo.
Amen.

Flemish

Onze Vader, die in de hemelen zijt,
uw naam worde geheiligd;
uw Koninkrijk kome;
uw wil geschiede gelijk in den hemel
alzo ook op de aarde;
geef ons heden ons dagelijks brood;
en vergeef ons onze schulden,
gelijk ook wij vergeven onzen schuldenaren;
en leid ons niet in verzoeking,
maar verlos ons van den booze;
Want uw is het Koninkrijk en de kracht
en de heerlijkheid in der eeuwigheid.
Amen.

Brazilian Portugese

Pai Nosso que estais nos céus,
santificado seja o vosso nome,
venha a nós o vosso reino,
seja feita a vossa vontade
assim na Terra como nos Céus.
O pão nosso de cada dia nos dai hoje,
perdoai as nossas ofensas
assim como nós perdoamos a quem nos tem ofendido,
não nos deixeis cair em tentação
e livrai-nos do mal.
Amén.

Croatian

Oce nas,
koji jesi na nebesima,
sveti se ime Tvoje,
dodji kraljevstvo Tvoje,
budi volja Tvoja kako na nebu tako i na zemlji.
Kruh nas svagdanji daj nam danas
i otpusti nam duge nase,
kako i mi otpustamo duznicima nasim,
i ne uvedi nas u napast,
nego izbavi nas od zla,
Amen.

French

Notre Père qui es aux cieux!
Que ton nom soit sanctifié;
que ton règne vienne;
que ta volonté soit faite sur la terre comme au ciel.
Donne-nous aujourd'hui notre pain quotidien;
pardonne-nous nos offenses,
comme nous aussi nous pardonnons à ceux qui nous ont
offensés;
ne nous induis pas en tentation,
mais délivre-nous du malin.
Car c'est à toi qu'appartiennent, dans tous les siècles,
le règne, la puissance et la gloire.
Amen!

Dutch

Onze Vader,
die in de hemelen zijt,
geheiligd zij Uw naam.
Uw rijk kome,
Uw wil geschiede op aarde als in de hemel.
Geef ons heden ons dagelijks brood,
en vergeef ons onze schulden,
gelijk ook wij vergeven aan onze schuldenaren.
En leid ons niet in bekoring,
maar verlos ons van het kwade.

Fijian

'Tama i keimami mai lomalagi,
Me vakarokorokotaki ma yacamuni.
Me yaco na nomuni lewa.
Me caka na lomamuni e vuravura
me vaka sa caka mai lomalagi.
Solia mai vei keimami e na
na siga oqo na kakana e yaga vei keimami.
Ia kakua ni cudruvi keikami e na vuku ni neimami
    valvala ca,
me vaka keimami sa sega ni cudruvi ira era sai valavala
    ca vei keimami.
Ia kakua ni kauti keimami ki na vere,
ka mo ni vakabulai keimami mai na ca:
Ni sa nomuni na lewa, kei na kaukauwa,
kei na vakarokoroko, ka sega ni mudu.
Emeni.

Catalan (Valenciano)

Pare nostre que esteu en el cel,
siga santificat el vostre nom,
vinga a nosaltres el vostre Regne,
faça's la vostra voluntat així a la terra com es fa en el cel;
el nostre pa de cada dia doneu-nos senyor el dia de hui,

i perdoneu les nostres culpes
així com nosaltres perdonem els nostres deutors
i no permeteu que nosatres caiguem a la tentació
ans allibereu-nos de qualsevol mal.
Amén.

Iraq *(Chaldean)*

Baban deele beshmaya,
payesh mkodsha shimukh, athya malkothokh,
hawe ojbonokh, dikh deele bishmaya hawe ham bara.
Halan lokhman sumqana dadyou.
Shwoq talan gnahan wkh-tiyathan,
dikh d-ham akhnee shwiqlan ta
ana dim-tu-dela ellan.
La mab-yeretan bjoraba,
ella mkhalislan min beesha,
bsabab deokh ela malkotha,
hela wtesh-bohta, laalam almeen,
Amen.

Luxembourg *(Letzeburesh)*

Eise Papp am Himmel,
däin Numm sief gehellégt.
Däi Räich soll kommen,
däi Wëll soll geschéien
wéi am Himmel sou op der Äerd.
Gëf äis haut eist deeglecht Brout,
verzei äis eis Schold,
wéi mir och dene verzeien,
déi an eiser Schold sin.
Féier äis nët an d'Versuchung,
mä maach äis fräi vum Béisen.
Amen.

Lithuanian

Teve Musu kuris esi dangujè!
Teesie šveñtas tàvo vardas,
teateinie tàvo karalyste,
Teesie tàvo valià
kaip danguje, taip ir zemeje.
Kasdienes musu dúonos dúok mùms šiañdien
ir atlèisk mums musu kaltès,
kaip ir mes atleidziame sàvo kaliniñkams.
Ir neléisk musu gùndyti,
bèt gélbek mùs nuo pikto.

Norway (Norsk)

Fader vår, du som er i himmelen!
Helliget vorde ditt navn;
komme ditt rike;
skje din vilje,
som i himmelen, så og på jorden;
gi oss idag vårt daglige brød;
og forlat oss vår skyld,
som vi og forlater våre skyldnere;
og led oss ikke inn i fristelse;
men fri oss fra det onde.
For riket er ditt,
og makten og æren i evighet.
Amen.

PRINCE KABOO

Sometime during 1872 in the forest of western Africa, Prince Kaboo was born to the chieftain of the Kru tribe. In this area tribes were constantly warring against one another and the defeated chieftain had to provide his eldest son as a hostage against payment of war debts to the victor. When Prince Kaboo was a teenager, the Kru tribe was defeated and Prince Kaboo's father could not satisfy the conqueror's demands. The enraged chieftain ordered Prince Kaboo to be whipped every day with a thorny, poison vine. When Prince Kaboo was thrown on a tree-made cross for his final beating, a great light appeared and a loud voice spoke out of the air telling Prince Kaboo to run. Miraculously healed in that instant, Prince Kaboo escaped into the jungle. Unable to return to his village, and unarmed and alone, he faced certain death in the deadly, dark jungle until a heavenly light showed the way to a settlement where he met his Deliverer and was born again.

Prince Kaboo was taken into a Methodist church and given the name, Samuel Morris. Morris had an intense drive to know more about the Holy Spirit, and decided to go to the United States to further his education. Morris didn't know that he was destined to become the first African missionary to the United States. With no money to pay for his passage, his simple faith in his heavenly Father led Morris to a ship's captain short of crew members.

Miraculously, the first person Morris met in New York took him directly to the Bethel mission maintained by the Revd Stephen Merritt. Merritt was leaving Bethel when, in halting English, Morris introduced himself, but promised to return and talk with him. Upon his return, Merritt found Morris on his knees praying, surrounded by 17 prostrate and weeping men who had just given their hearts to God.

As Morris and Merritt talked about the Spirit-filled life, Merritt discovered that he was the one being taught by the unassuming young man who would be called 'the apostle of simple faith'. Merritt, feeling that Morris needed an education to fulfil his calling, sent Morris to a friend who was the president of Taylor University. The university was enthralled with Morris. Wherever Morris was, as he began to pray the Holy Spirit would descend and believers and unbelievers alike would fall to their knees.

Samuel Morris died at 21 years of age, during the severe winter of 1893. The impact of his life moved organizations and people. Through his influence, a lukewarm, American university caught fire with a vision for lost souls and missions and, over the next several years, many were called to be Morris' replacement in Africa and other parts of the world. Morris' story was translated into five languages and became a rallying point for men called to missions around the world.

THE DEAD SEA SCROLLS

The phrase, 'Dead Sea Scrolls', has become the standard designation for the more than 850 documents discovered in 11 caves near the ancient ruins of Qumran (Israel) between 1947 and 1956. The Scrolls appear to be part of a sacred library of a Jewish sect known as the Essenes. Little is known about this group apart from that recorded by the Jewish historian Josephus. He notes that the Essenes were a messianic, 'new covenant' group led by a priest called the 'Teacher of Righteousness'.

Following the accidental discovery of seven scrolls kept in clay jars by a Bedouin shepherd boy, interest in these documents has been intense. The Dead Sea Scrolls, made from animal skins, papyrus and copper, can broadly be categorized into biblical and non-biblical documents.

The biblical scrolls contain fragments of every book in the Old Testament (except Esther), including:

- At least 19 copies of the book of Isaiah
- 25 copies of Deuteronomy
- 30 copies of Psalms

Other, non-biblical scrolls include:

- The book of Enoch
- Stories about Noah and Abraham
- Psalms attributed to David and Joshua
- Wisdom writings
- Liturgies
- Hymns
- Benedictions

- Commentaries on Habakkuk, Nahum and Hosea
- The last words of Joseph, Judah, Levi, Naphtali and Amram (the father of Moses)

Interestingly, the Scrolls confirm that the Masoretic Text, used as a foundation for many Bible translations, is substantially accurate. However, as much as 30 per cent of the Scrolls have not yet been published and thus, Bible scholars are keen to see further evidence of the integrity of the Old Testament.

The famous 4Q285 fragment known as the 'Pierced Messiah' text, is of particular fascination to Bible scholars. It is a six-line statement, written in a Herodian script of the first half of the first century, and refers to a Messiah from the Branch of David, to a judgement and to a killing.

1. Isaiah the prophet: [The thickets of the forest] will be cut [down
2. with an axe and Lebanon by a majestic one will f]all. And there shall come forth a shoot from the stump of Jesse [
3. the Branch of David and they will enter into judgement with [
4. and the Prince of the Congregation, the Bran[ch of David] will kill him [
5. by stroke]s and by wounds. And a Priest [of renown (?)] will command [
6. the s]lai[n] of the Kitti[m]

The major documents from these finds are now housed in Jerusalem in a special museum called the Shrine of the Book.

Scrolls similar to the Dead Sea Scrolls have also been discovered at Masada, the Herodian site occupied by Jewish zealots in AD 70 after the fall of Jerusalem.

COLLECTIONS OF PAPYRI

Ancient manuscripts of the Bible are much prized and collectors have spent many year and millions of pounds in preserving these much-loved documents. Among the most famous papyri manuscripts are:

Collection Name	Abbreviation	Description
Amherst Papyri	P.Amh.	Belongs to the Right Hon. Lord Amherst of Hackney. Includes 'The Ascension of Isaiah' and other biblical and early Church fragments, as well as other classical documents from the Ptolemaic, Roman, and Byzantine eras.
Bodmer Papyri	P.Bod.	These Greek and Coptic documents were discovered in Egypt, probably at Pabau, near a Pachomian monastery. Approximately 50 manuscripts was purchased by M. Martin Bodmer of Switzerland in 1955–6.

Collection Name	Abbreviation	Description
Chester Beatty Papyri	P. Chester Beatty	These manuscripts date from the second to the fourth centuries. Eleven codices was acquired by Alfred Chester Beatty, an American, in 1930–1 and 1935. The collection is housed near Dublin, Ireland, in the Chester Beatty Library and Gallery of Oriental Art. The Chester Beatty Library website is located at: www.cbl.ie
Colt Papyri	P.Colt	Located at Pierpont Morgan Library (New York).
Egerton Papyrus 2	P.Eg.	The first four fragments from an early papyrus codex were discovered in 1934 among miscellaneous scraps purchased from an antiquities dealer. Their provenance is unknown, but may be Oxyrhynchus, Egypt.

Collection Name	Abbreviation	Description
Michigan Papyri	P.Mich.	Over 10,000 papyrus fragments (with 7,000 separate inventory numbers) are housed at the University of Michigan
Oxyrhynchus Papyri	P.Oxy.	Discovered by Bernard P. Grenfell and Arthur S. Hunt, beginning in 1897 in and around Oxyrhynchus (modern Behnesa), Egypt, located about 125 miles south of Cairo. Owned by a variety of libraries, universities and museums.
Princeton Papyri	P.Princ.	Located at Princeton University, New Jersey.
Rylands Papyri	P.Ryl.	Collection of ancient Greek resources includes over seven hundred papyri, in addition to 31 ostraca and 54 codices. These date from the third century. Located in the John Rylands Library at the University of Manchester.

KIDS' BIBLE HOWLERS

In the first book of the Bible, Guinessis, God got tired of creating the world, so he took the Sabbath off.

Adam and Eve were created from an apple tree.

Noah's wife was called Joan of Ark.

Noah built an ark, which the animals come on to in pears.

Lot's wife was a pillar of salt by day, but a ball of fire by night.

Samson was a strong man who let himself be led astray by a Jezebel like Delilah.

Samson slayed the Philistines with the axe of the Apostles.

Moses led the Hebrews to the Red Sea, where they made unleavened bread which is bread without any ingredients.

The Egyptians were all drowned in the dessert.

Afterwards, Moses went up on Mount Cyanide to get the ten amendments.

The first commandment was when Eve told Adam to eat the apple.

The fifth commandment is to humour thy father and mother.

The seventh commandment is thou shalt not admit adultery.

Moses died before he ever reached Canada.

The greatest miracle in the Bible is when Joshua told his son to stand still and he obeyed him.

David was a Hebrew king skilled at playing the liar.

Solomon, one of David's sons, had 300 wives and 700 porcupines.

When Mary heard that she was the mother of Jesus, she sang the Magna Carta.

[87]

When the three wise guys from the east side arrived, they found Jesus in the manager.

Jesus was born because Mary had an immaculate contraption.

Jesus enunciated the Golden Rule, which says to do one to others before they do one to you.

He also explained, 'a man doth not live by sweat alone'.

It was a miracle when Jesus rose from the dead and managed to get the tombstone off the entrance.

The people who followed the Lord were called the 12 decibels.

The epistles were the wives of the apostles.

One of the opossums was St Matthew who was also a taximan.

St Paul cavorted to Christianity. He preached holy acrimony, which is another name for marriage.

A Christian should have only one spouse. This is called monotony.

BIBLE FIRST AID KIT

Ailment	Solution

Trouble or sorrow	Even though I walk
	    through the valley of the shadow
	of death,
	I will fear no evil,
	    for you are with me;
	your rod and your staff,
	    they comfort me. (Psalm 23.4)

Slipped down and hurt yourself	'Because you love me,' says the
	LORD, 'I will rescue you;
	    I will protect you, for you
	acknowledge my name.
	You will call upon me, and I will
	answer you; I will be with you in
	trouble,
	    I will deliver you and honour
	you. (Psalm 91.14–15)

Feeling lonely and burdened	Come to me, all you who are weary and burdened, and I will give you rest. Take my yoke upon you and learn from me, for I am gentle and humble in heart, and you will find rest for your souls. (Matthew 11.28–29)
Loss of memory	Praise the LORD, O my soul, and forget not all his benefits. (Psalm 103.2)
Failing strength	Be strong and courageous. (Joshua 1.7)
Weak faith	Hebrews 11

Ailment	Solution
Guilt	That you may know that the Son of Man has authority on earth to forgive sins. (Mark 2.10)
Pride	When pride comes, then comes disgrace, but with humility comes wisdom. (Proverbs 11.2)
Foolishness	Wise men store up knowledge, but the mouth of a fool invites ruin. (Proverbs 10.14)
Hate	The righteous hate what is false, but the wicked bring shame and disgrace. (Proverbs 13.5)
Temptation	God is faithful; he will not let you be tempted beyond what you can bear. But when you are tempted, he will also provide a way out so that you can stand up under it. (1 Corinthians 10.13)
Lying	The LORD detests lying lips, but he delights in men who are truthful. (Proverbs 12.22)
Fear	So do not fear, for I am with you; do not be dismayed, for I am your God. (Isaiah 41.10)
Anxiety	Do not be anxious about anything, but in everything, by prayer and petition, with thanksgiving, present your requests to God. (Philippians 4.6)

HOW TO REMEMBER THE NAMES OF THE TWELVE APOSTLES

Of all the Twelve Apostles,
The Gospels give the names:
First, *Andrew*, *John* and *Peter*,
Bartholomew and *James*,
Matthew, *Simon* and *Thomas*
Were friends tried and true.
Then *Philip*, *James* and *Thaddeus*,
The traitor *Judas* too.
They followed Christ the Master
O'er mountain, shore and sea,
Throughout Samaria, Judea, Perea, and Galilee.

BIBLE HEROES – WILLIAM TYNDALE (1492–1536)

'I had perceived by experience, how that it was impossible to stablish the lay people in any truth, except the Scripture were plainly laid before their eyes in their mother tongue, that they might see the process, order, and meaning of the text.' William Tyndale, Preface to the Pentateuch, 1530

Sir Frederic G. Kenyon in the Dictionary of the Bible edited by James Hastings, and published by Charles Scribner's Sons of New York in 1909.

Gloucestershire-born William Tyndale was an Oxford and Cambridge scholar who devoted his life to translating the Bible into English. Before his English translation was published in

1525, the Bible was not readily understood by the common people because it was still in Latin.

In 1524 Tyndale left England on his mighty mission. He settled in the free city of Hamburg and had knowledge of the German reformer, Martin Luther. Tyndale was a brilliant and diligent scholar and during his year in Hamburg, he finished his translation of the New Testament. Three thousand copies were produced in Cologne and gradually made their way to England.

The church authorities were outraged by Tyndale's efforts since they perceived a loss of power and prestige if the Scriptures could be read by the common people. King Henry VIII, Sir Thomas More, Cardinal Wolsey, and numerous bishops demanded the burning of the Tyndale Testament. Indeed, copies were burnt at St Paul's Cross in London.

But Tyndale had lit a torch of his own for such was the demand for his translation that no sooner had the authorities confiscated and destroyed copies than other copies appeared on the market. The appetite for an English Bible was huge and some clergymen, including Archbishop Warham, although against Tyndale's Testament, nevertheless sought the King's favour to produce a New Testament in English approved by the Church of England.

Tyndale used Luther's German translation and Desiderius Erasmus' translation of 1522 as the basis for his work, but he sought to be guided by God in producing a faithful translation. Following the success of his New Testament, in 1530 Tyndale produced a translation of the Pentateuch, the only remaining copy of which is held in the British Musuem. A year later he translated the book of Jonah and in 1534 revised his New Testament, a copy of which was presented to Anne Boleyn. Before his martyrdom he also completed translations from Joshua to Chronicles. Copies of both are now in the British Museum.

In 1535, he was hard at work revising his earlier New Testament translations, when he was betrayed by Henry Phillips, an imperial spy who pretended to be a Bible student. He was tried and found guilty of heresy at Vilvorde Castle in Brussels and on 6 October 1536 he was strangled at the stake and afterwards his body was burnt.

Tyndale was the greatest force of the English Reformation and his translation was the foundation for the 1611 Authorized Version. His last great cry was, 'Lord, open the King of England's eyes.'

Here are the first few verses of Genesis from the Tyndale Bible:

> *In the beginning God created heaven and earth.*
> *The earth was void and empty, and darkness was upon the deep, and the spirit of God moved upon the water.*
> *Then God said: let there be light and there was light.*
> *And God saw the light that it was good: and divided the light from the darkness,*
> *and called the light day, and the darkness night: and so of the evening and morning was made the first day.*
> *And God said: let there be a firmament between the waters, and let it divide the waters asunder.*
> *Then God made the firmament and parted the waters which were under the firmament, from the waters that were above the firmament: And it was so.*
> *And God called the firmament heaven. And so of the evening and morning was made the second day.*
> *And God said let the waters that are under heaven gather themselves unto one place, that the dry land may appear: And it came so to pass.*

BIBLE HEROES – JOHN WYCLIF (1320–84)

The first Bible to be produced in the English language was translated into English by Oxford theologian John Wyclif, who wrote the text out by hand in the 1380s. Wyclif, knowing no Hebrew or Greek, translated from the Latin Vulgate. He was accused of heresy and excommunicated by the Roman

Catholic Church, but continued with his task until his death in 1384. Every copy of his translation had to be written out by hand, but so many copies were produced that a Bill was enacted in Parliament to forbid the translation's circulation.

Archbishop Arundel complained to the Pope of 'that pestilent wretch Wyclif'. The convocation of Oxford under Arundel in 1408 decreed 'that no man hereafter by his own authority translate any text of the Scripture into English or any other tongue, by way of book, pamphlet or treatise; and that no man read any such book, pamphlet or treatise, now lately composed in the time of John Wyclif or since . . . publicly or privately upon pain of greater excommunication. He that shall do contrary to this shall likewise be punished as a favourer of heresy and error.'

The Pope was so infuriated by his teachings that he ordered his body to be exhumed, his bones crushed and scattered in a river. During the next hundred years many Christian martyrs were burned to death with Wyclif's Bible tied around their necks, but over 100 copies are still in existence.

Today, the Wyclif Foundation, named in his honour, is committed to translating the Bible into all the languages spoken anywhere in the world.

It shall greatly helpe ye to understande Scripture,
If thou mark not only what is spoken or wrytten,
But of whom,and to whom,
With what words,at what time
Where,to what intent,
With what circumstances,
Considering what goeth before
And what followeth.

John Wyclif

H. B. Workman, *John Wyclif: A Study of the English Medieval Church*, 2 vols, 1926

JOHN NELSON DARBY (1800–82)

John Nelson Darby, an Anglo-Irish Bible teacher and founder of the Plymouth Brethren published translations of the Bible in French and German from 1890. This is an extract from his preface to *Synopsis to the Books of the Bible*:

> Deeply convinced of the divine inspiration of the scriptures, given to us of God, and confirmed in this conviction by daily and growing discoveries of their fullness, depth, and perfectness; ever more sensible, through grace, of the admirable perfection of the parts, and the wonderful connection of the whole, the writer only hopes to help the reader in the study of them.
>
> The scriptures have a living source, and living power has pervaded their composition: hence their infiniteness of bearing, and the impossibility of separating any one part from its connection with the whole, because one God is the living centre from which all flows; one Christ, the living centre round which all its truth circles, and to which it refers, though in various glory; and one Spirit, the divine sap which carries its power from its source in God to the minutest branches of the all-united truth, testifying of the glory, the grace, and the truth of Him whom God sets forth as the object and centre and head of all that is in connection with Himself, of Him who is, withal, God over all, blessed for evermore.
>
> To give all this as a whole and perfectly would require the Giver Himself. Even in learning it, we know in part, and we prophesy in part. The more – beginning from the utmost leaves and branches of this revelation of the mind of God, by which we have been reached when far from Him – we have traced it up towards its centre, and thence looked down again towards its extent and diversity, the more we learn its infiniteness and our own feebleness of apprehension. We learn, blessed be God, this, that the love which is its source is found in unmingled perfectness and fullest display in those manifestations of it which have reached us

even in our ruined state. The same perfect God of love is in it all. But the unfoldings of divine wisdom in the counsels in which God has displayed Himself remain ever to us a subject of research in which every new discovery, by increasing our spiritual intelligence, makes the infiniteness of the whole, and the way in which it surpasses all our thoughts, only more and more clear to us. But there are great leading principles and truths, the pointing out of which in the various books which compose the scriptures, may assist in the intelligence of the various parts of scripture. It is attempted to do this here. What the reader is to expect, consequently, in this Synopsis, is nothing more than an attempt to help him in studying scripture for himself. All that would turn him aside from this would be mischievous to him; what helps him in it may be useful. He cannot even profit much by the following pages otherwise than in using them as an accompaniment to the study of the text itself.

CREEDS

Creed \'kreed\: ME crede, *from* OE creeda, *from Latin* credo ('I believe' the first word of the Apostles' and Nicene creeds), *from* credere *to believe, trust, entrust; akin to OIr* cretid 'he believes'
1: *a brief authoritative formula of religious belief*
2: *a set of fundamental beliefs*
3: *a guiding principle*

The Apostles' Creed

Legend has it that the Apostles wrote this creed on the tenth day after Christ's ascension into heaven. It is the most popular creed used in worship by Western Christians. Its central doctrines are those of the Trinity and God the Creator.

I believe in God, the Father almighty,
creator of heaven and earth.
I believe in Jesus Christ, God's only Son, our Lord,
who was conceived by the Holy Spirit,
born of the Virgin Mary,
suffered under Pontius Pilate,
was crucified, died, and was buried;
he descended to the dead.
On the third day he rose again;
he ascended into heaven,
he is seated at the right hand of the Father,
and he will come again to judge the living and the dead.
I believe in the Holy Spirit,
the holy catholic church,
the communion of saints,
the forgiveness of sins,
the resurrection of the body,
and the life everlasting.
Amen.

English Language Liturgical Consultation

The Nicene Creed

The Nicene Creed was originally the result of the Council of Nicea in AD 325. While there are similarities between the text of the Nicene Creed and the text of the Apostles' Creed, the Nicene Creed is more definite and explicit than the Apostles' Creed in the statement of the divinity of Christ and the Holy Spirit. The Nicene Creed provided the needed clarification to combat the heresies of the Nicene age, and is useful to combat those same heresies today which invariably reoccur in differing forms.

I believe in one God, the Father Almighty,
Maker of heaven and earth,
and of all things visible and invisible.
And in one Lord Jesus Christ,

the only-begotten Son of God, begotten of the Father before all worlds;

God of God, Light of Light, very God of very God;

begotten, not made, being of one substance with the Father,

by whom all things were made.

Who, for us men for our salvation, came down from heaven,

and was incarnate by the Holy Ghost of the virgin Mary, and was made man;

and was crucified also for us under Pontius Pilate;

He suffered and was buried;

and the third day He rose again, according to the Scriptures;

and ascended into heaven, and sits on the right hand of the Father;

and He shall come again, with glory, to judge the quick and the dead;

whose kingdom shall have no end.

And I believe in the Holy Ghost,

the Lord and Giver of Life; who proceeds from the Father and the Son;

who with the Father and the Son together is worshipped and glorified;

who spoke by the prophets.

And I believe one holy catholic and apostolic Church.

I acknowledge one baptism for the remission of sins;

and I look for the resurrection of the dead, and the life of the world to come.

Amen.

Book of Common Prayer

The Athanasian Creed

The Athanasian Creed is noted for its strong focus on the doctrine of the Trinity.

Whosoever will be saved, before all things it is necessary that he hold the catholic faith. Which faith except everyone do keep whole and undefiled, without doubt he shall perish everlastingly. And the catholic faith is this: That we worship one God in Trinity, and Trinity in Unity, neither confounding the persons, nor dividing the substance.

For there is one Person of the Father, another of the Son, and another of the Holy Ghost. But the godhead of the Father, of the Son, and of the Holy Ghost, is all one, the glory equal, the majesty co-eternal.

Such as the Father is, such is the Son, and such is the Holy Ghost. The Father uncreated, the Son uncreated, and the Holy Ghost uncreated. The Father incomprehensible, the Son incomprehensible, and the Holy Ghost incomprehensible.

The Father eternal, the Son eternal, and the Holy Ghost eternal. And yet they are not three eternals, but one Eternal.

As also there are not three incomprehensibles, nor three uncreated, but one Uncreated, and one Incomprehensible. So likewise the Father is Almighty, the Son Almighty, and the Holy Ghost Almighty. And yet they are not three almighties, but one Almighty.

So the Father is God, the Son is God, and the Holy Ghost is God. And yet they are not three gods, but one God.

So likewise the Father is Lord, the Son Lord, and the Holy Ghost Lord. And yet not three lords, but one Lord.

For as we are compelled by the Christian verity to acknowledge each Person by himself to be both God and Lord, so we are also forbidden by the catholic religion to say that there are three gods or three lords.

The Father is made of none, neither created, nor begotten. The Son is of the Father alone, not made, nor created, but begotten. The Holy Ghost is of the Father, neither made, nor created, nor begotten, but proceeding.

[99]

So there is one Father, not three fathers; one Son, not three sons; one Holy Ghost, not three holy spirits.

And in the Trinity none is before or after another; none is greater or less than another, but all three Persons are co-eternal together and co-equal. So that in all things, as is aforesaid, the Unity in Trinity and the Trinity in Unity is to be worshipped.

He therefore that will be saved must think thus of the Trinity.

Furthermore, it is necessary to everlasting salvation that he also believe rightly the Incarnation of our Lord Jesus Christ. For the right faith is, that we believe and confess, that our Lord Jesus Christ, the Son of God, is God and man; God, of the substance of the Father, begotten before the worlds; and man of the substance of his mother, born in the world; perfect God and perfect man, of a rational soul and human flesh subsisting. Equal to the Father, as touching his godhead; and inferior to the Father, as touching his manhood; who, although he is God and man, yet he is not two, but one Christ; one, not by conversion of the godhead into flesh but by taking of the manhood into God; one altogether; not by confusion of substance, but by unity of person. For as the rational soul and flesh is one man, so God and man is one Christ; who suffered for our salvation, descended into hell, rose again the third day from the dead. He ascended into heaven, he sits at the right hand of the Father, God Almighty, from whence he will come to judge the quick and the dead. At his coming all men will rise again with their bodies and shall give account for their own works. And they that have done good shall go into life everlasting; and they that have done evil into everlasting fire.

This is the catholic faith, which except a man believe faithfully, he cannot be saved.

Book of Common Prayer

The following Scripture passages are examples of declarations of faith from the Bible:

Hear O Israel, the Lord is our God, the Lord is one.

Deuteronomy 6.4

When all the people saw this, they fell prostrate; and cried, 'The Lord, he is God; the Lord, he is God.'

1 Kings 18.39

Simon Peter answered, 'You are the Christ, the Son of the living God.'

Matthew 16.16

Therefore go and make disciples of all nations, baptizing them in the name of the Father and of the Son and of the Holy Spirit.

Matthew 28.19

Then Nathanael declared, 'Rabbi, you are the Son of God; you are the King of Israel!'

John 1.49

Simon Peter answered him, 'Lord to whom shall we go? You have the words of eternal life. We believe, and know that you are the Holy One of God.'

John 6.68–69

Thomas said to him, 'My Lord and my God!'

John 20.28

As they travelled along the road they came to some water, and the eunuch said, 'Look, here is water. Why shoudn't I be baptized?' And Philip said, 'If you believe with all your heart, you may.' The eunuch answered, 'I believe that Jesus Christ is the Son of God.'

Acts 8.36–37

They replied, 'Believe in the Lord Jesus, and you will be saved – you and your household.'

Acts 16.31

Yet for us there is one God, the Father, from whom are all things and for whom we live, and there is but one Lord, Jesus Christ, through whom all things came and through whom we live.

1 Corinthians 8.6

Therefore I tell you that no one who is speaking by the Spirit of God says 'Jesus be cursed!' and no one can say 'Jesus is Lord' except by the Holy Spirit.

1 Corinthians 12.3

What I received I passed on to you as of first importance, that Christ died for our sins according to the Scriptures, that he was buried, that he was raised on the third day according to the Scriptures, and that he appeared to Peter, then to the Twelve. After that he appeared to more than five hundred of the brothers at the same time, most of whom are still living, though some have fallen asleep. Then he appeared to James, then to all the apostles.

1 Corinthians 15.3–7

Who, though he was in the form of God, did not consider equality with God something to be grasped, but made himself nothing, taking the very nature of a servant, being born in the likeness of men. And being found in human form he humbled himself and became obedient to death, even death on a cross! Therefore God exalted him to the highest place and gave him the name that is above every name, that at the name of Jesus every knee should bow, in heaven and on earth and under the earth, and every tongue confess that Jesus Christ is Lord, to the glory of God the Father.

Philippians 2.6–11

Beyond all question the mystery of godliness is great. He appeared in a body, was vindicated by the Spirit, was seen by angels, was preached among the nations, was believed on in the world, was taken up in glory.

1 Timothy 3.16

Therefore let us leave the elementary teachings about Christ and go on to maturity, not laying again the foundation of repentance from acts that lead to death, and of faith in God, instruction about baptisms, the laying on of hands, the resurrection of the dead, and eternal judgement.

Hebrews 6.1–2

This is how you can recognize the Spirit of God. Every spirit that acknowledges that Jesus Christ has come in the flesh is from God.

1 John 4.2

LECTIO DIVINA

Lectio Divina (Latin, lek-see-o de-vee-na) is a way of praying and reading the Bible that originated with St Benedict of Nursia (*c.* 480–*c.* 547). The father of Western monasticism established a Bible-based series of principles for holy living, known as a Rule that is observed by followers of the Benedictine Order to this day. Lectio Divina is incorporated into the Rule of St Benedict.

Lectio Divina is often translated as 'meditative or spiritual reading' and can be thought of as praying with a listening heart. Monks and nuns pray for many hours every day and use the Lectio Divina as a way of structuring their prayers and helping them to be centred on the Scriptures.

The main principles of this method are:

Preparation

Place   Find a time and place where you can be quiet.
Posture Be relaxed and comfortable, but stay alert, not sleepy!
Passage Think about the passage you have chosen before you begin.
Prayer   Ask the Holy Spirit to help you understand his word.

Practice

Lectio	Read the passage slowly. Pause when you feel your attention drawn to a word, phrase or thought.
Meditatio	Ponder this passage and what it means for you. Write down your thoughts as you listen to the leading of the Spirit.
Oratio	Prayer. Talk with God about the passage and your reflection.
Contemplatio	When moved by God, rest in the quiet presence of God; surrender to grace. When ready, return to your reading.

NEW TESTAMENT BOOKS AND EARLY WRITERS

Contrary to modern opinion, the books of the New Testament were widely recognized as part of the Word of God from the earliest times. The table below shows the remarkable degree of agreement between leading biblical authorities of their time.

Italic type indicates that the writer either does not mention the book or expressed some doubt about the status of the book.

Athanasius (b. 296)	Origen (b. 185)	Irenaeus (b. 130)
Matthew	Matthew	Matthew
Mark	Mark	Mark
Luke	Luke	Luke
John	John	John
Acts	Acts	Acts
Romans	Romans	Romans
1 Corinthians	1 Corinthians	1 Corinthians

2 Corinthians	2 Corinthians	2 Corinthians
Galatians	Galatians	Galatians
Ephesians	Ephesians	Ephesians
Philippians	Philippians	Philippians
Colossians	Colossians	Colossians
1 Thessalonians	1 Thessalonians	1 Thessalonians
2 Thessalonians	2 Thessalonians	2 Thessalonians
1 Timothy	1 Timothy	1 Timothy
2 Timothy	2 Timothy	2 Timothy
Titus	Titus	Titus
Philemon	Philemon	Philemon
Hebrews	Hebrews	*Hebrews*
James	*James*	*James*
1 Peter	1 Peter	1 Peter
2 Peter	*2 Peter*	*2 Peter*
1 John	1 John	1 John
2 John	*2 John*	*2 John*
3 John	*3 John*	*3 John*
Jude	*Jude*	*Jude*
Revelation**	Revelation	Revelation

**The Revelation of John was first received and then rejected by many churches in Asia Minor.

CRUCIFIXION – A MEDICAL VIEW

Crucifixion was one of the most horrendous, shameful and painful ways to die. The Roman Empire refined this cruel method of punishment, so that by the time of Jesus' death, it was the worst suffering known to man. This is an account of the medical effects of crucifixion:

1. The cross is placed on the ground and the exhausted man is quickly thrown backwards with his shoulders against the wood.
2. The legionnaire feels for the depression at the front of the

wrist. He drives a heavy, square wrought iron nail through the wrist deep into the wood.

3. Quickly he moves to the other side and repeats the action, being careful not to pull the arms too tightly, but to allow some flex and movement.

4. The cross is then lifted into place.

5. The left foot is pressed backwards against the right foot, and with both feet extended, toes down, a nail is driven through the arch of each, leaving the knees flexed. The victim is now crucified.

6. As he slowly sags down with more weight on the nails in the wrists, excruciating fiery pain shoots along the fingers and up the arms to explode in the brain.

7. The nails in the wrists are putting pressure on the median nerves. As he pushes himself upward to avoid this stretching torment, he places the full weight on the nail through his feet. Again he feels the searing agony of the nail tearing through the nerves between the bones of his feet.

8. As the arms fatigue, cramps sweep through his muscles, knotting them in deep relentless, throbbing pain. With these cramps comes the inability to push himself upward to breathe.

9. Air can be drawn into the lungs but not exhaled. He has to raise himself in order to get even one small breath.

10. Finally, carbon dioxide builds up in the lungs and in the bloodstream, and the cramps partially subside. Spasmodically, he is able to push himself upward to exhale and bring in life-giving oxygen.

11. Hours of limitless pain, cycles of twisting, joint wrenching cramps, intermittent partial asphyxiation, searing pain as tissue is torn from his lacerated back as he moves up and down against rough timber.

12. Then another agony begins: a deep, crushing pain deep in the chest as the pericardium slowly fills with serum and begins to compress the heart. It is now almost over. The loss of tissue fluids has reached a critical level – the compressed heart is struggling to pump heavy, thick, sluggish blood into the tissues – the tortured lungs are making a

frantic effort to gasp in small gulps of air. He can feel the chill of death creeping through his tissues.

13. Finally, he can allow his body to die . . . All this . . . the Bible records with the simple words, 'and they crucified him' (Mark 15.24). What wondrous love is this?

Scripture tells us that although the agony of the physical punishment upon the cross was great, crucifixion did not kill Jesus – 'No one takes it (my life) from me, but I lay it down of my own accord' (John 10.18).

THE JEFFERSON BIBLE

Thomas Jefferson (1743–1826), the principal author of the Declaration of Independence, believed that the teachings of Jesus were immensely valuable, but he did not believe in the miracles of the New Testament. So, he compiled his own 'Bible' that extracted Jesus' parables and other teaching but ignored the supernatural element. He told his friend and rival John Adams that he was rescuing the philosophy of Jesus and the 'pure principles which he taught', from the 'artificial vestments in which they have been muffled by priests, who have travestied them into various forms as instruments of riches and power for themselves'. After having selected from the evangelists 'the very words only of Jesus', he believed 'there will be found remaining the most sublime and benevolent code of morals which has ever been offered to man'.

Jefferson's 'Bible' was called, *The Life and Morals of Jesus of Nazareth Extracted Textually from the Gospels*. It was published in 1804 and followed up in 1820 by a more ambitious work called, *The Life and Morals of Jesus of Nazareth Extracted Textually from the Gospels in Greek, Latin, French and English*.

The Jefferson Bible has no account of the Annunciation, no Virgin Birth, no shepherds or angels at the Nativity, no mention of the Trinity and no account of the resurrection.

To Jefferson, Jesus was a superb moral teacher whose message was based on absolute love and service. He was not the Son of God, the Messiah or the Saviour of Mankind, but a wonderful teacher whose moral example showed us how to live.

The Jefferson Bible is comprised of 17 chapters with extracts from the four Gospels.

BIBLE HEROES – NOAH WEBSTER (1758–1843)

America's greatest lexicographer Noah Webster was born in West Hartford, Connecticut in 1758. He is famous today as the author of two valuable reference sources, the English language *Compendious Dictionary*, published in 1806 (followed by an *American Dictionary of the English Language*, published in 1828) and the first American colonial Bible, published in 1833.

His dictionary introduced American spellings for English words so that 'musick' became 'music', 'centre' became 'center', 'colour' became 'color' and 'plough' became 'plow'. His dictionary had more than 70,000 words in it (including 12,000 new words) and it quickly became a best seller, second only to the Bible.

Webster based his Bible translation on the King James Version and it took many years before his Bible was accepted because of the popularity of the King James Version.

Webster had a brilliant intellect that mastered twenty languages including Chaldean, Syriac, Hebrew, Arabic, Ethiopic and Persian. He also produced a popular spelling book for schools called the *Blue Backed Speller* and spent many years promoting the federal cause. In 1831 Congress adopted his American dictionary as the national standard for spelling and definition.

This is an extract from the preface of Webster's Bible:

In this country there is no legislative power which claims to have the right to prescribe what version of the Scriptures shall be used in the churches, or by the people. And as all human opinions are fallible, it is doubtless for the interest of religion that no authority should be exerted in this case, except by commendation.

At the same time, it is very important that all denominations of Christians should use the same version, that in all public discourses, treatises and controversies, the passages cited as authorities should be uniform. Alterations in the popular version should not be frequent; but the changes incident to all living languages render it not merely expedient, but necessary at times to introduce such alterations as will express the true sense of the original languages, in the current language of the age. A version thus amended may require no alteration for two or three centuries to come.

In this undertaking, I subject myself to the charge of arrogance; but I am not conscious of being actuated by any improper motive. I am aware of the sensitiveness of the religious public on this subject; and of the difficulties which attend the performance. But all men whom I have consulted, if they have thought much on the subject, seem to be agreed in the opinion, that it is high time to have a revision of the common version of the Scriptures; although no person appears to know how or by whom such revision is to be executed. In my own view, such revision is not merely a matter of expedience, but of moral duty; and as I have been encouraged to undertake this work by respectable literary and religious characters, I have ventured to attempt a revision upon my own responsibility. If the work should fail to be well received, the loss will be my own, and I hope no injury will be done. I have been painfully solicitous that no error should escape me. The reasons for the principal alterations introduced, will be found in the explanatory notes.

The Bible is the chief moral cause of all that is good, and the best corrector of all that is evil in human society; the best book for regulating the temporal concerns of men, and the only book that can serve as an infallible guide to future felicity. With this estimate of its value, I have attempted to render the English version more useful, by correcting a few obvious errors, and removing some obscurities, with objectionable words and phrases; and my earnest prayer is that my labors may not be wholly unsuccessful.

THE BIBLE ON 'LOVE'

Love is the most written about, sung about, agonized about, cherished and philosophized about subject in the world. Naturally, the Bible has much to say on love.

God is love (1 John 4.8) and by the Holy Spirit he makes his love reside in us (Romans 5.5). God so loved the world that he sent his only Son so that we might not perish but have eternal life (John 3.16). Love is the highest human experience, greater than faith and hope (1 Corinthians 13.13). Love is kind, enduring, always hopes, always believes, always rejoices in truth and is long-suffering (1 Corinthians 13). Perfect love is the antidote to fear (1 John 4.8) and the covering for a multitude of sins (1 Peter 4.8).

Love is not boastful, rude, self seeking, evil, envious, easily provoked or proud (1 Corinthians 13). Love seeks no ill to its neighbour, does not rejoice in iniquity, never fails and abides forever (1 Corinthians 13).

Nothing can separate us from the love of God; not death nor life, not angels or principalities or powers, not the past or the future, not height nor depth or any other creature in creation (Romans 8.38–9).

Love is commanded by the Lord (John 13.34) and when we live in love we show we follow his commandments (2 John 6). Love is the way to spiritual gifts such as prophecy, discernment, faith and self-sacrifice (1 Corinthians 13).

Love is the fulfilment of the law (Romans 13.10) and the bond of perfection (Colossians 3.14).

THE WESTMINSTER CONFESSION OF FAITH

An extract from the 1646 Westminster Confession of Faith:

CHAPTER I

Of the Holy Scripture

I. Although the light of nature, and the works of creation and providence, do so far manifest the goodness, wisdom, and power of God, as to leave men inexcusable; yet are they not sufficient to give that knowledge of God, and of his will, which is necessary unto salvation; therefore it pleased the Lord, at sundry times, and in divers manners, to reveal himself, and to declare that his will unto his Church; and afterwards for the better preserving and propagating of the truth, and for the more sure establishment and comfort of the Church against the corruption of the flesh, and the malice of Satan and of the world, to commit the same wholly unto writing; which maketh the Holy Scripture to be most necessary; those former ways of God's revealing his will unto his people being now ceased.

II. Under the name of Holy Scripture, or the Word of God written, are now contained all the Books of the Old and New Testament, which are these:

Of the Old Testament

Genesis
Exodus
Leviticus
Numbers
Deuteronomy
Joshua
Judges
Ruth
I Samuel
II Samuel
I Kings
II Kings
I Chronicles
II Chronicles
Ezra
Nehemiah
Esther
Job
Psalms
Proverbs

Ecclesiastes
The Song of Songs
Isaiah
Jeremiah
Lamentations
Ezekiel
Daniel
Hosea
Joel
Amos
Obadiah
Jonah
Micah
Nahum
Habakkuk
Zephaniah
Haggai
Zechariah
Malachi

Of the New Testament

The Gospels according to
    Matthew
    Mark
    Luke
    John
The Acts of the Apostles
Paul's Epistles to the Romans
Corinthians I
Corinthians II
Galatians
Ephesians
Philippians
Colossians
Thessalonians I

Thessalonians II
Timothy I
Timothy II
Titus
Philemon
The Epistle to the
    Hebrews
The Epistle of James
The First and Second
    Epistles of Peter
The First, Second and
    Third Epistles of John
The Epistle of Jude
The Revelation

All which are given by inspiration of God, to be the rule of faith and life.

[112]

BIBLE NUMBERS – 1

One is the first cardinal number and scripturally signifies *unity* and *primacy*. It excludes all difference and denotes that which is sovereign:

In the Bible, God is *first*, and before all:

> This is what the LORD says –,
> Israel's King and Redeemer, the LORD Almighty:
> I am the first, and I am the last;
> apart from me there is no God. (Isaiah 44.6)

> Listen to me, O Jacob, Israel, whom I have called;
> I am he; I am the first and I am the last.
> My own hand laid the foundations of the earth,
> And my right hand spread out the heavens.
> (Isaiah 48.12–13)

> The LORD will be king over the whole earth. On that day there will be *one* LORD, and his name the only name.
> (Zechariah 14.9)

> There is *one* body and one Spirit – just as you were called to *one* hope when you were called – *one* Lord, *one* faith, *one* baptism; *one* God and Father of all, who is over all and through all and in all. (Ephesians 4.4–6)

First recorded words of Jesus:

> 'Why were you searching for me?' he asked. 'Didn't you know I had to be in my Father's house?' (Luke 2.49)

Words that appear only *once* in the Bible:

Critic – Hebrews 4.12

To corrupt – 2 Corinthians 2.17

To handle deceitfully – 2 Corinthians 4.2

Perfect – 2 Timothy 3.17

Expressly – 1 Timothy 4.1

To bewitch – Galatians 3.1

Daily (*epiousios*) – Matthew 6.11

A thorn – 2 Corinthians 12.7

Overseer (*allotrio-episkopos*) – 1 Peter 4.15

Twelve tribes – (Acts 26.7)

Preaching – Jonah 3.2,

Forgetfulness – Psalm 88.12

BIBLE NUMBERS – 2

As opposed to one, the number 2 signifies *division* or *difference*, especially enmity:

Do *two* walk together unless they have agreed to do so? (Amos 3.3)

This is the word that came to Jeremiah from the LORD: 'Go down to the potter's house, and there I will give you my message.' So I went down to the potter's house, and I saw him working at the wheel. But the pot he was shaping from the clay was marred in his hands; so the potter formed it into *another* pot, shaping it as seemed best to him. (Jeremiah 18.1–4)

On the *second* day of creation, God said, 'Let there be an expanse between the waters to separate water from water.' (Genesis 1.6)

Two Covenants

The first of Law, is superseded (Hebrews 8.7, 8, 13; 10.9) by the second 'better Covenant' (Hebrews 8.6, 8; 10.9, 16, 17).

The *ordinances* of the Law, 'weak' and 'unprofitable' (Hebrews 7.18; 10.6, 9). The ordinances of grace, the 'good things to come'.

'The *first man*', marred (Genesis 2.7; 3.19), and of the earth, earthy. 'The second man', the Lord from Heaven (1 Corinthians 15.47). The first Adam condemned to death, the last Adam living again for evermore.

The *body*, marred in the Fall, and made subject to death and corruption, but in resurrection to be made like Christ's own body of glory (1 John 3.1–3; Philippians 3.21; Romans 8.23; 1 Corinthians 15.42–49).

Notable Twos

Abraham and Lot
Isaac and Ishmael
Jacob and Esau
David and Jonathan
James and John
Peter and Andrew
Paul and Barnabas

BIBLE NUMBERS – 3

Three denotes *completeness,* as three lines complete a plane figure. Hence, three is significant of *divine perfection* and completeness. The third day completes the fundamentals of creation work.

> And God said, 'Let the water under the sky be gathered to one place, and let dry ground appear.' And it was so. God called the dry ground 'land', and the gathered waters he called 'seas'. And God saw that it was good. Then God said, 'Let the land produce vegetation: seed-bearing plants and trees on the land that bear fruit with seed in it, according to their various kinds.' And it was so. The land produced vegetation: plants bearing seed according to their kinds and trees bearing fruit with seed in it according to their kinds. And God saw that it was good. And there was evening, and there was morning – the *third* day. (Genesis 1.9–13)

Three, therefore, stands for that which is solid, real, substantial, complete and entire.

All things that are specially complete are stamped with this number three.

God's principal attributes are three: omniscience, omnipresence and omnipotence.

There are three great divisions completing time – past, present and future.

Thought, word and deed complete the sum of human capability.

Three propositions are necessary to complete the simplest form of argument – the major premise, the minor and the conclusion.

Three kingdoms embrace our ideas of matter – mineral, vegetable and animal.

In the Bible, this completion becomes divine, and marks divine completeness or perfection.

Three is the number associated with the Godhead, for there are 'three persons in one God'. Three Persons of the Trinity:

Ephesians 3.19, The fullness of God.
Ephesians 4.13, The fullness of Christ.
Colossians 2.9, The fullness of the Godhead.

Three times the Seraphim cry, 'Holy, Holy, Holy' – one for each of the three Persons in the Trinity (Isaiah 6.3). Three times is the blessing given in Numbers 6.23, 24:
'The LORD bless thee and keep thee (the Father);
The LORD make his face shine upon thee; and be gracious unto thee (the Son);
The LORD lift up his countenance upon thee, and give thee peace' (the Holy Spirit).

Book of Common Prayer

The measurements of the Holy of Holies, which was the central and highest place of worship, formed a perfect cube.

Three is a number of resurrection, for it was on the third day that Jesus rose again from the dead. This was divine in operation, and divine in its prophetic foreshowing in the person of Jonah (Matthew 12.39, 40; Luke 11.29; Jonah 1.17). It was for three hours (from the sixth to the ninth) that darkness shrouded the Divine Sufferer and Redeemer.

Divine perfections of Christ:

- 'The Spirit, the water and the blood', are the divinely perfect witness to the grace of God on earth (1 John 5.7).
- The three years of his seeking fruit testifies to the completeness of Israel's failure (Luke 13.7).
- His threefold 'it is written' shows that the Word of God is the perfection of all ministry (Matthew 4).
- He raised three persons from the dead.
- The inscriptions on the cross in three languages show the completeness of his rejection by man.
- He is Prophet, Priest and King, raised up from among his brethren (Deuteronomy 17.15; 18.3–5 and 18.15).
- He 'has appeared', 'now appears in Heaven' and shall 'appear again' (Hebrews 9.26, 28).

BIBLE NUMBERS – 4

If 1 symbolizes unity and 3 symbolizes divine perfection then their product – 4 – symbolizes God's creative works. On the fourth day of creation, the sun, moon and stars were created, signifying the completion of God's material work (aside from biological life).

Thus there are:

- Four great elements – earth, air, fire and water
- Four Gospels
- Four regions of the earth – north, south, east and west
- Four divisions of the day – morning, noon, evening and midnight
- Four seasons of the year – spring, summer, autumn and winter
- Four great variations of lunar phases
- Four materials of the Tabernacle, three being metals (gold, silver, brass) and one non-metal (wood)
- Four coverings of the Tabernacle, – three animal (goats' hair, rams' skins, and badger skins) and one vegetable (fine linen)
- The ornamentations of the curtains were four – three being colours (blue, purple and scarlet); while one was a pattern (the cherubim)
- The Manna (Exodus 16.14, 31) has a fourfold description, three referring to sight or appearance (small, white, round) and one to taste (sweet)
- Four houses were built by Solomon; three were for himself, – his own house (1 Kings 7.1), the house of the forest of Lebanon (v. 2), the house for Pharaoh's daughter (v. 8) while one was the House of the LORD (1 Kings 6.37)
- God's four judgments in the earth (Ezekiel 14.21) – three are inanimate (the sword, famine and pestilence) while one is animate (the noisome beast).

The body is sown and raised (1 Corinthians 15.42–44) in three ways that relate to corruptibility:

- sown 'in corruption, raised in incorruption';
- sown 'in dishonour, raised in glory';
- sown 'in weakness, raised in power';
- while in the one, 'it is sown a natural body; it is raised a spiritual body'.

In the parable of the sower (Matthew 13) there are four kinds of soil; but three are characterized as being all alike in contrast to the one (the wayside, the stony ground and the thorns). These are all unprepared while the one is good because it is prepared.

In the story of Daniel, there are four young men of Israel:

- Daniel [alone]
- Shadrach [together]
- Meshach [together]
- Abednego [together]

In the Lost Son's welcome (Luke 15), three things were material (the robe, the ring and the shoes); while one was spiritual (the kiss).

'The Seventy' went forth with a fourfold prohibition (Luke 10.4), of which three related to matters (carry no purse, no scrip, no shoes), while one related to action ('salute no man by the way').

God's fourfold witness in the earth (Hebrews 2.4): three are impersonal (signs, wonders and miracles), and one personal (the gifts of the Holy Spirit).

The fulness of material blessing in the earth is described in Isaiah 60.17: 'Instead of bronze I will bring you gold, and silver in place of iron. Instead of wood I will bring you bronze, and iron in place of stones.'

BIBLE NUMBERS – 5

The number 5 signifies divine grace.

By God's Grace:

- Israel came out of Egypt in ranks of five.
- David had five smooth stones in his encounter with Goliath.
- The promise of God to Israel in Leviticus 26 is 'I will grant peace in the land, and you will lie down and no one will make you afraid. I will remove savage beasts from the land, and the sword will not pass through your country. You will pursue your enemies, and they will fall by the sword before you. Five of you will chase a hundred, and a hundred of you will chase ten thousand, and your enemies will fall by the sword before you.'
- Paul's preference was to 'speak five words with understanding, than ten thousand words in an unknown tongue' (1 Corinthians 14.19).
- The holy anointing oil for the consecration of the Tabernacle and its priests had five ingredients according to Exodus 30: myrrh, sweet cinnamon, sweet calamus, cassia and olive oil.
- Similarly the holy incense had five ingredients: frankincense, stacte, onycha, galbanum and salt.

BIBLE NUMBERS – 6

Six denotes the man and human effort.

Man was created on the sixth day, and thus he has the number six impressed upon him. Moreover, six days were appointed to him for his labour. Six also represents falling short of God's perfection since Man is born into sin and under God's wrath.

The enemy of God, symbolized by a serpent, is given six names:

1. Nachash, a shining one (Genesis 3.1; Job 26.13)
2. Ak-shoov, meaning 'to bend back' or 'lie in wait', translated adder, Psalm 140.3
3. Ephah, any poisonous serpent, translated adder; also viper (Job 20.16; Isaiah 30.6, 59.5)
4. Tsiph-ohnee, a small hissing serpent or viper (Isaiah 11.8, 59.5; Proverbs 23.32)
5. Tanneen, a great serpent, or dragon on account of its length (Exodus 7.9, 10, 12)
6. Saraph, from the root 'to burn'; a venomous, deadly serpent, from the heat and inflammation caused by its bite. (Numbers 21.8; Isaiah 14.29, 30.6)

Nehemiah was hindered in his work for God in six ways:

1. Grief (2.10)
2. Laughter (2.19)
3. Wrath, indignation and mocking (4.1–4)
4. Fighting and open opposition (4.7, 8)
5. False meeting (6.1, 2)
6. False friends (6.10–14)

Six times Jesus was charged with being demon-possessed:

1. 'He is possessed by Beelzebub.' (Mark 3.22, and Matthew 12.24)

2. 'You are demon-possessed.' (John 7.20)
3. 'Aren't we right in saying that you are ... demon-possessed?' (John 8.48)
4. 'Now we know that you are demon-possessed.' (John 8.52)
5. 'He hath a devil, and is mad.' (John 10.20)
6. 'He casteth out devils by Beelzebub.' (Luke 11.15)

Six times Jesus was asked for a sign, by:

1. The Pharisees (Matthew 12.38; Mark 8:11)
2. The Sadducees (Matthew 16.1)
3. The disciples (Matthew 24.3; Mark 13.4)
4. The people (Luke 11.16)
5. The Jews (John 2.18)
6. The people (John 6.30)

BIBLE NUMBERS – 7

Seven is a wonderful number in the Bible for it denotes spiritual perfection. If the sixth day of creation is of man and labour, the seventh is of rest. As such, seven represents God's perfection and blessing.

Abraham's sevenfold blessing in Genesis 12.2–3:

I will make you a great nation,
And I will bless you,
I will make your name great;
And you will be a blessing;
I will bless those who bless you,
And whoever curses you I will curse:
And all peoples on earth will be blessed through you.

God's sevenfold blessing upon Israel in Exodus 6.6–8:

I will bring you out from Egypt.
I will free you from being slaves.
I will redeem you.
I will take you as my own people.
I will be your God.
I will bring you in to the land.
I will give it you.

On the day of Atonement, the High Priest sprinkled the blood in a sevenfold blessing:

On the mercy-seat (Leviticus 16.14).
Before the mercy-seat (Leviticus 16.14).
Before the veil (Leviticus 4.17).
On the horns of the golden altar (Exodus 30.10).
On the horns of the brazen altar (Leviticus 16.18).
Round about upon the altar (Leviticus 16.19).
At the foot of the brazen altar (Leviticus 4.18).

Seven miracles in John's Gospel:

> The water turned into wine (ch. 2)
> The nobleman's son (4.47)
> At the pool of Bethesda (5.4)
> The feeding of the 5,000 (ch. 6)
> The man born blind (9.1)
> The raising of Lazarus (ch. 11)
> The draught of fishes (ch. 21)

Other examples of the significance of the number 7 include:

- The seven gifts of Romans 12.6–8
- The seven unities of Ephesians 4.4–6
- The seven characteristics of wisdom, James 3.17
- The seven titles of Christ in Hebrews:

> Heir of all things, 1.2
> Captain of our salvation, 2.10
> Apostle, 3.1
> Author of salvation, 5.9
> Forerunner, 6.20
> High Priest, 10.21
> Author and finisher of faith, 12.2

MORE BIBLE NUMBERS

Numbers are used in Scripture, not merely as in Nature, with *supernatural design,* but with *spiritual significance,* which may be summarized as follows:

Eight denotes *resurrection, regeneration*; a new beginning or commencement. The eighth is a new first. Hence the octave in music, colour, days of the week, etc. It is the number which has to do with the Lord, who rose on the eighth, or new 'first day'. This is, therefore, the *Dominical* number.

Nine denotes *Finality of judgement.* It is 3 × 3, the product of divine completeness. The number nine, or its factors or multiples, is seen in all cases when *judgement* is the subject.

Ten denotes *Ordinal perfection.* Another new first; after the ninth digit. When numeration commences anew. Noah completed the antediluvian age in the tenth generation from God.

Eleven denotes *disorder, disorganization,* because it is one short of the number 12. Jacob had 11 sons who were in peril until the revelation of the twelfth, Joseph.

Twelve denotes *Governmental perfection.* It is the number or factor of all numbers connected with government: whether by tribes or apostles, or in measurements of time, or in things which have to do with government in the heavens and the earth.

Thirteen denotes *rebellion, apostasy, defection, disintegration, revolution,* etc. The first occurrence fixes this (Genesis 14.4) and the second confirms it (Genesis 17.25)

Seventeen denotes a combination of *spirit* and *order* (10 + 7). Romans 8.35–39 is a list of 17 things that will not separate us from God's love: tribulation, distress, persecution, famine, nakedness, peril, sword, death, life, angels, principalities, powers, things present, things to come, height, depth or any other creature.

Forty – denotes *trial and chastisement*. Moses had to wait 40 years before he could lead the children of Israel. He was on Mount Sinai for 40 days meeting with God. Israel were in the desert for 40 years. Jesus was tempted by the Devil for 40 days and appeared to his disciples for 40 days following his resurrection.

E. W. Bullinger, *Number in Scripture*,
Eyre and Spottiswode, London 1921.

SIMON GREENLEAF (1783–1853)

American jurist, Simon Greenleaf was one of the founding fathers of Harvard Law School and taught there as the Royall Professor of Law. He has been described as a brilliant lawyer and the highest authority in American courts.

Greenleaf's most famous work, *A Treatise on the Law of Evidence*, is still considered to be the greatest single authority on evidence in the entire literature of legal procedure.

A noted agnostic, Greenleaf set out to disprove the authenticity of the Bible. He brought his clear legal mind to the task and an impartial attitude. He studied the Bible for evidence of error or myth but found none and had to conclude it was the divine word of God. In particular, he was impressed with the detailed description of the trial, sentence and resurrection of Jesus recorded in the Gospels.

In his work entitled *Examination of the Testimony of the Four Evangelists by the Rules of Evidence Administered in Courts of Justice, with an Account of the Trial of Jesus*, Simon Greenleaf stated:

> The Character they portrayed is perfect. It is the character of a sinless Being – One supremely wise and supremely good . . .

The doctrines and precepts of Jesus are in strict accordance with the attributes of God, agreeable to the most exalted ideas which we can form of them, from reason or revelation. They are strictly adapted to the capacities of mankind, and yet are delivered with a simplicity wholly Divine. 'He spake as never man spake.' He spake with authority, yet addressed himself to the reason and understanding of men, and he spake with wisdom which men could neither gainsay nor resist.

In reference to the apostles, Greenleaf concluded:

They had every possible motive to review carefully the grounds of their faith, and the evidences of the great facts and truths which they asserted . . . And their writings show them to have been men of vigorous understandings. If then, their testimony was not true, there was no possible motive for this fabrication.

In correspondence with the American Bible Society, Cambridge, 6 November 1852, Simon Greenleaf wrote:

Of the Divine character of the Bible, I think, no man who deals honestly with his own mind and heart can entertain a reasonable doubt, For myself, I must say, that having for many years made the evidences of Christianity the subject of close study, the result has been a firm and increasing conviction of the authenticity and plenary inspiration of the Bible. It is indeed the Word of God.

THE BIBLE ON 'FAITH'

Faith comes 'from hearing the message, and the message is heard through the word of Christ' (Romans 10.17). The Bible defines faith as 'being sure of what we hope for and certain of what we do not see' (Hebrews 11.1). This chapter is known as the 'highway of faith' because it lists many wonderful examples of what can be achieved through faith. By faith:

- We understand that the universe was formed at God's command, so that what is seen was not made out of what was visible.
- Abel offered God a better sacrifice than Cain did. By faith he was commended as a righteous man, when God spoke well of his offerings. And by faith he still speaks, even though he is dead.
- Enoch was taken from this life, so that he did not experience death; he could not be found, because God had taken him away.
- Noah, when warned about things not yet seen, in holy fear built an ark to save his family. By his faith he condemned the world and became heir of the righteousness that comes by faith.
- Abraham, when called to go to a place he would later receive as his inheritance, obeyed and went, even though he did not know where he was going.
- Isaac blessed Jacob and Esau in regard to their future.
- Jacob, when he was dying, blessed each of Joseph's sons, and worshipped as he leaned on the top of his staff.
- Joseph, when his end was near, spoke about the exodus of the Israelites from Egypt and gave instructions about his bones.
- Moses' parents hid him for three months after he was born, because they saw he was no ordinary child, and they were not afraid of the king's edict.
- Moses, when he had grown up, refused to be known as the son of Pharaoh's daughter. He chose to be mistreated along

with the people of God rather than to enjoy the pleasures of sin for a short time.

• The prostitute Rahab, because she welcomed the spies, was not killed with those who were disobedient.

How much faith is required? 'If you have faith as small as a mustard seed, you can say to this mulberry tree, "Be uprooted and planted in the sea," and it will obey you' (Luke 17.6). The Gospel reveals, 'a righteousness from God, a righteousness that is by faith from first to last, just as it is written: "The righteous will live by faith"' (Romans 1.17). Faith is a gift of the Holy Spirit (1 Corinthians 12.9) and Christians are encouraged to 'live by faith, not by sight' (2 Corinthians 5.7).

Faith is eternal, for 'these three remain: faith, hope and love. But the greatest of these is love' (1 Corinthians 13.13). The only thing that counts is faith expressing itself through love (Galatians 5.6)

In contrast, 'the Spirit clearly says that in later times some will abandon the faith and follow deceiving spirits and things taught by demons' (1 Timothy 4.1). Also, 'without faith it is impossible to please God, because anyone who comes to him must believe that he exists and that he rewards those who earnestly seek him' (Hebrews 11.6).

BIBLE HEROES – REUBEN ARCHER TORREY (1856–1928)

Dr R. A. Torrey, for many years the associate to the great evangelist Dwight L. Moody, was one of the great Christian leaders of his era. He was educated at Yale and also at various German universities. During his early years he went through a time of extreme scepticism, but emerged as a staunch preacher of the faith.

He was the second president of the Moody Bible Institute, succeeding its founder in 1899. He wrote many books addressing the fundamentals of the Christian faith, including *How to Pray*, *The Deity of Jesus Christ*, *How to Work for Christ* and *How to be Inexpressibly Happy*. He listed the following principles to be used for a proper understanding of the Bible from his book, *The Importance and Value of Proper Bible Study*.

- Get absolutely right with God yourself by the absolute surrender of your will to him.
- Be determined to find out just what God intended to teach and not what you wish him to teach.
- Get the most accurate text.
- Find the most exact and literal meaning of the text.
- Note the exact force of each word used.
- Interpret the words used in any verse according to Bible usage.
- Interpret the words of each author in the Bible with a regard to the particular usage of that author.
- Interpret individual verses with a regard to the context.
- Interpret individual passages in the light of parallel or related passages.
- Interpret obscure passages in the light of passages that are perfectly plain.

- Interpret any passage in the Bible as those who were addressed would have understood it.
- Interpret what belongs to the Christian as belonging to the Christian; what belongs to the Jew, as belonging to the Jew, and what belongs to the Gentiles, as belonging to the Gentiles.
- Interpret each writer with a view to the opinions the writer opposed.
- Interpret poetry as poetry and interpret prose as prose.
- The Holy Spirit is the best interpreter of the Bible.

BIBLE WEIGHTS AND MEASURES

Unit	Imperial	Metric
Weight		
talent	75 pounds	34 kilograms
mina	1¼ pounds	0.6 kilogram
hekel (2 bekas)	⅖ ounce	11.5 grams
pim (⅔ shekel)	⅓ ounce	7.6 grams
bekah (10 gerahs)	⅕ ounce	5.5 grams
gerah	1/50 ounce	0.6 gram
Dry Capacity		
cor (homer) (10 ephahs)	6 bushels	220 litres
lethek (5 ephahs)	3 bushels	110 litres
ephah (10 omers)	⅗ bushel	22 litres
seah (⅓ ephah)	7 quarts	7.3 litres
Omer (1/10 ephah)	2 quarts	2 litres
Cab (1/18 ephah)	1 quart	1 litres

Unit	Imperial	Metric
Liquid Capacity		
bath (1 ephah)	6 gallons	22 litres
hin (⅙ bath)	4 quarts	4 litres
log (1/72 bath)	⅓ quart	0.3 litres
Length		
cubit	18 inches	0.5 meter
span	9 inches	23 centimetres
handbreadth	3 inches	8 centimetres

Note: These figures are based upon the best, conservative information available, however, it is not possible to be precise.

BIBLE ORGANIZATIONS

Across the globe many organizations have been established to ensure translation and distribution of the Bible. This is a list of the prominent Bible organizations that are reaching out to many nations with the word of God:

Organization	Brief details
Gideons International	Founded in 1899, in America, to 'win men, women, boys and girls to the Lord Jesus Christ', this non-profit organization freely distributes one million copies of the Word of God every week.
Bible League	Founded in Chicago in 1936. Work with local churches in more than 50 countries, teaching them to draw seekers into Bible studies. In 2004 Christians trained by the Bible League gathered 2,685,594 people into small group Bible studies.

Book of Hope	Established in 1987 by missionary evangelist Bob Hoskins. The Book of Hope publication contains the four Gospels. The publication was first distributed to the children and young people of El Salvador, but is now available across the world in over 65 languages. In 2005 the 300 millionth copy was given to Deyse Souza, a 14-year-old Brazilian girl.
HOSANNA/ Faith Comes By Hearing	Founded in 1972 to make every translation of the Bible available in audio form, in every church or village in the world, so that all people, especially the 50 per cent of the world who cannot read, can hear God's Word in the language they pray in.
Institute for Bible Translation	Started in 1973 to translate and publish the Bible in the languages of non-Slavic peoples living in Russia and other countries of the Commonwealth of Independent States.
International Bible Society	Founded in 1809 in New York to 'extend the knowledge of the Holy Scripture . . . persuaded that a more extensive distribution among persons who are destitute of them will have by the divine blessing more beneficial effects'. So far over 400 million people have been provided with Scriptures from the International Bible Society.

Life Publishers International	Began in Missouri 1946 as the Spanish Literature Division of the Assemblies of God. Changed name in 1966 to 'Editorial Vita' and moved to Miami. Changed name again in 1980 to current name and today is based in Springfield, Missouri.
Lutheran Bible Translators (LBT)	Founded in 1964 by Dr Morris and Lois Watkins in California. Support over 80 LBT missionaries and operate in 18 countries.
New Tribes Mission	Began in 1942 by Paul Fleming to disciple believers, translate the Scriptures, and train teachers and leaders to tribal peoples in 18 countries across the world.
Open Doors International	Started in 1955 through the call of God to one man, Brother Andrew. Provides Bibles and Christian literature to the persecuted Church.
Pioneer Bible Translators	Provide Bibles in the mother tongue, to establish indigenous churches and train leaders for God.
Scripture Gift Mission	Produce contemporary and accessible Bible-based resources for people all around the world in nearly 200 languages. Last year, Scripture Gift Mission supplied over 7 million Bibles, many of them in the poorest countries of the world.

Scripture Union International	Begun in the beach-side town of Llandudno, Wales in 1867 by Josiah Spiers. He wanted children to know God's love and began by writing 'God is Love' in the sand. As children gathered around, he encouraged them to decorate the letters with shells and seaweed and told them stories about Jesus. Today, Scripture Union operates in nearly 130 countries.
United Bible Societies	An alliance of over 140 national Bible Societies working in over 200 countries.
World Bible Translation Center	Exists to translate and distribute faithful, easy-to-understand translations of the Scriptures in the world's major languages to lead people to Jesus and help believers grow in faith. In 2004 WBTC distributed over 3.4 million Scriptures, including 128,000 Bibles, 563,000 New Testaments, 2,174,000 Scripture portions and 586,000 Internet downloads in 28 languages.

THE FATE OF THE APOSTLES

Scripture does not record how the Apostles died, but tradition holds that they were all martyred or banished, as victims of Roman persecution:

Peter	Crucified upside down in Rome in AD 66
Andrew	Crucified in AD 74
James, son of Zebedee	Beheaded in Jerusalem in AD 44
James, son of Alphaeus	Beaten to death in AD 60
John the Beloved	Banished to the Isle of Patmos in AD 96
Philip	Crucified in Phrygia in AD 52
Bartholomew	Crucified in AD 52
Thomas	Run through by a lance in India in AD 52
Matthew	Slain with a sword in Ethiopia in AD 60
Simon	Crucified in Persia in AD 74
Mark	Died in Alexandria after being dragged through the streets
Thaddeus	Shot by arrows in AD 72
Paul	Beheaded in Rome in AD 66
Barnabas	Stoned to death in Salonica
Luke	Hanged on an olive tree in Greece

BIBLE TERMS FOR SIN

What is sin? The Bible uses many different terms to cover the basic tendency to do wrong inherent in every person. The Bible provides a comprehensive explanation for the existence of sin and how we can be set free from it now and for evermore. Here are some Bible terms for this much misunderstood and sorry state:

- The Old Testament has at least eight Hebrew words to describe sin – *ra* meaning 'bad', *rasha* meaning 'wickedness', *asham* meaning 'guilt', *chata* meaning 'sin', *avon* meaning 'iniquity', *shagag* meaning 'err', *taah* meaning 'wander away' and *pasha* meaning 'rebel'. Perhaps the last term best describes the overall 'drive' of sin – it is rebellion against that which is right and true.
- The New Testament has at least 11 Greek terms to describe sin, including *kakos* meaning 'bad', *poneros* meaning 'evil', *absebes* meaning 'godless', *enochos* meaning 'guilt', *adikia* meaning 'unrighteousness', *agnoein* meaning 'ignorant', *anomos* meaning 'lawlessness', *parabtes* meaning 'transgression', *planan* meaning 'to go astray', *paratoma* meaning 'to fall away' and *hupocrites*, meaning 'hypocrite'.

The Bible does not make a distinction between serious (mortal) and not so serious (venial) sins, although the Catholic Church teaches this as one of its doctrines. The remedy of salvation by faith in Jesus, based upon the grace of God, saves sinners from the penalty, power and presence of sin.

These truths are admirably expressed in Charles Wesley's popular hymn, 'Ye Ransomed Sinners Hear':

> Ye ransomed sinners, hear,
> The prisoners of the Lord;
> And wait till Christ appear
> According to his Word.
> Rejoice in hope; rejoice with me.
> Rejoice in hope; rejoice with me.

We shall from all our sins be free.
In God we put our trust:
If we our sins confess,
Faithful he is, and just,
From all unrighteousness
To cleanse us all, both you and me;
To cleanse us all, both you and me.

We shall from all our sins be free.
Surely in us the hope
Of glory shall appear;
Sinners, your heads lift up
And see redemption near.
Again I say: rejoice with me.
Again I say: rejoice with me.

THE RIGHTEOUS AND THE WICKED COMPARED IN PROVERBS 10

- *Proverbs10.3* – The LORD does not let the righteous go hungry, but he thwarts the craving of the wicked.
- *Proverbs10.6* – Blessings crown the head of the righteous, but violence overwhelms the mouth of the wicked.
- *Proverbs10.7* – The memory of the righteous will be a blessing, but the name of the wicked will rot.
- *Proverbs10.8* – The wise in heart accept commands, but a chattering fool comes to ruin.
- *Proverbs10.9* – The man of integrity walks securely, but he who takes crooked paths will be found out.
- *Proverbs10.11* – The mouth of the righteous is a fountain of life, but violence overwhelms the mouth of the wicked.
- *Proverbs 10.14* – Wise men store up knowledge, but the mouth of a fool invites ruin.

- *Proverbs 10.16* – The wages of the righteous bring them life, but the income of the wicked brings them punishment.
- *Proverbs 10.20* – The tongue of the righteous is choice silver, but the heart of the wicked is of little value.
- *Proverbs 10.21* – The lips of the righteous nourish many, but fools die for lack of judgement.
- *Proverbs 10.27* – The fear of the LORD adds length to life, but the years of the wicked are cut short.
- *Proverbs 10.28* – The prospect of the righteous is joy, but the hopes of the wicked come to nothing.

THE AITKEN BIBLE

Robert Aitken, a book publisher from Edinburgh, went to Philadelphia in 1769 to seek his fortune. Because of the bitter relations between Britain and America, Bibles were hard to import and Aitken, a keen Quaker, seized on the idea of producing an American Bible.

On 21 January 1781 Aitken petitioned the US Congress with an offer to 'print a neat edition of the Holy Scriptures for use in schools'. His request was granted and what became known as the 'Bible of the American Revolution' (in the King James Version) was available to everyone. Ten thousand copies of his Bible were produced and it remains the only Bible formally approved by Congress!

This is the text of Aitken's petition:

To the Honourable The Congress of the United States of America The Memorial of Robert Aitken of the City of Philadelphia, Printer Humbly Sheweth
That in every well regulated Government in Christendom The Sacred Books of the Old and New Testament, commonly called the Holy Bible, are printed and published under the Authority of the Sovereign Powers, in order to prevent the fatal confusion that would arise, and the alarming

Injuries the Christian Faith might suffer from the Spurious and erroneous Editions of Divine Revelation. That your Memorialist has no doubt but this work is an Object worthy the attention of the Congress of the United States of America, who will not neglect spiritual security, while they are virtuously contending for temporal blessings. Under this persuasion your Memorialist begs leave to, inform your Honours That he both begun and made considerable progress in a neat Edition of the Holy Scriptures for the use of schools, But being cautious of suffering his copy of the Bible to Issue forth without the sanction of Congress, Humbly prays that your Honours would take this important matter into serious consideration & would be pleased to appoint one Member or Members of your Honourable Body to inspect his work so that the same may be published under the Authority of Congress. And further, your Memorialist prays, that he may be commissioned or otherwise appointed & Authorized to print and vend Editions of, the Sacred Scriptures, in such manner and form as may best suit the wants and demands of the good people of these States, provided the same be in all things perfectly consonant to the Scriptures as heretofore Established and received amongst us.

COMPARING CALVINISM AND ARMINIANISM

Calvinism and Arminianism are two theological positions that take their names from the two men associated with their development, though they were not the sole proponents of each.

John Calvin, was born in 1509 and died in 1564. He was a pastor in Geneva and along with Martin Luther in Germany, was the most influential force in the Protestant Reformation. In Basel, Switzerland, Calvin published the first edition of his *Institutes of the Christian Religion* (1536). He firmly believed that the Bible taught predestination: the belief that God has foreordained all things, and especially that God has elected certain souls to eternal salvation. However, by 1538, Genevan leaders reacted against the doctrines of the Protestant pastors and Calvin and several other clergymen were banished. That same year, Calvin became the pastor of a church in Strasbourg, Germany. Later, the Geneva city council begged Calvin to return and he did in 1541. Incidentally, Calvin was a great municipal leader improving Geneva's hospitals, schools and sewers.

Dutch theologian Jacobus Arminius (1560–1609), a professor of theology at the University of Leiden, Holland, was born only four years before the death of John Calvin. He argued against the Calvinistic views on predestination. Arminius' followers published the *Remonstrance*, a formal reproof or complaint against Calvinism, to the Synod of Dordt in 1610. This Synod was a national assembly and council made up of 84 Dutch theologians and 18 commissioners who met and agreed that Arminius' teachings were unbiblical.

The different positions of the two camps are summarized below in terms of their stance on major isses:

Issue	Calvinist position	Arminian position
Original sin	*Total depravity* and guilt inherited from Adam	*Weakness* inherited from Adam
Grace of God	*Unconditional grace.* Common grace given to all; saving grace given to elect	*Enabling grace* given to all; saving grace given to those who believe; persevering grace given to those who obey

Issue	Calvinist position	Arminian position
Extent of Atonement	*Limited Atonement.* Intended only for the elect	*Unlimited.* Intended for all
Predestination	*Irresistible grace.* Rooted in God's decrees	Rooted in God's *foreknowledge*
Perseverance	*Perseverance of all* the elect by the grace of God	Perseverance *dependent* on obedience
Human will	In *bondage* to sin	*Free* to do spiritual good
Regeneration	Monergistic – solely the work of *God*	*Synergistic* – Man is involved
Atonement	Christ's death a *substitutionary* penal sacrifice	Christ's death a sacrifice that God benevolently accepted in *place of a penalty*
Application of atonement	By power of the Holy Spirit according to the *will of God*	By power of the Holy Spirit in response to the *will of the sinner*
Order of salvation	*Election, predestination*, union with Christ, calling, regeneration, faith, repentance, justification, sanctification, glorification	*Calling*, faith, repentance, regeneration, justification, perseverance, glorification

BIBLICAL INERRANCY

Def: *Inerrant* (n): *considered accurate, truthful, reliable, totally free of error, without mistake and absolutely authoritative.*

Summary of the 1978 Chicago Statement of the International Council on Biblical Inerrancy:

1. God, who is himself Truth and speaks truth only, has inspired Holy Scripture in order thereby to reveal himself to lost mankind through Jesus Christ as Creator and Lord, Redeemer and Judge. Holy Scripture is God's witness to himself.

2. Holy Scripture, being God's own Word, written by men prepared and superintended by his Spirit, is of infallible divine authority in all matters upon which it touches: It is to be believed, as God's instruction, in all that it affirms; obeyed, as God's command, in all that it requires; embraced, as God's pledge, in all that it promises.

3. The Holy Spirit, Scripture's divine Author, both authenticates it to us by his inward witness and opens our minds to understand its meaning.

4. Being wholly and verbally God-given, Scripture is without error or fault in all its teaching, no less in what it states about God's acts in creation, about the events of world history, and about its own literary origins under God, than in its witness to God's saving grace in individual lives.

5. The authority of Scripture is inescapably impaired if this total divine inerrancy is in any way limited of disregarded, or made relative to a view of truth contrary to the Bible's own; and such lapses bring serious loss to both the individual and the Church.

APOCRYPHAL BOOKS

The brilliant Bible scholar, St Jerome first used the Greek term 'apocrypha', meaning 'hidden things' to refer to texts included in the Septuagint (the Greek version of the Old Testament), but not in the Hebrew Bible.

There has been much debate about the number and names of the Apocryphal books and over the centuries various Bible versions have included or omitted some or all of these texts. Protestant churches generally exclude the apocrypha (though the King James version of 1611 included them). The Roman Catholic and Orthodox churches include all of the Old Testament Apocrypha, sometimes referring to them as 'deutero-canonical' (second canon) books. These books are also referred to as the 'pseudepigrapha' by some Protestant churches.

The Apocryphal Books include:

• The First Book of Adam and Eve
• The Second Book of Adam and Eve
• The Apocalypse of Adam
• The Second Treatise of the Great Seth
• 1 Enoch
• 2 Enoch
• Melchizedek
• The Book of Abraham
• The Testament of Abraham
• Joseph and Aseneth
• The Book of Moses
• The Martyrdom of Isaiah
• The Ascension of Isaiah
• The Revelation of Esdras
• The Book of Jubilees
• Tales of the Patriarchs
• The Letter of Aristeas
• The Book of the Apocalypse of Baruch
• The Greek Apocalypse of Baruch

- 1 Esdras
- 2 Esdras
- 1 Maccabees
- 2 Maccabees
- 3 Maccabees
- 4 Maccabees
- The Letter of Jeremiah
- The Prayer of Azariah
- Baruch
- The Prayer of Manassas
- Bel and the Dragon
- Wisdom of Sirach
- Wisdom of Solomon
- Additions to Esther
- Tobit
- Judith
- Susanna
- Psalm 151
- Epistle of the Apostles
- History of Joseph the Carpenter
- Apocryphon of James
- The Letter of Peter to Philip
- Book of John the Evangelist
- Avenging of the Saviour
- The Sentences of Sextus
- Book of Thomas the Contender
- The Lost Gospel According to Peter
- The Last Gospel of Peter
- Gospel of Bartholomew
- Gospel of Thomas
- Gospel of Philip
- Secret Gospel of Philip
- Secret Gospel of Mark
- Paul and Seneca

FLORA IN THE BIBLE

Song of Songs 2.12: 'Flowers appear on the earth; the season of singing has come'

Plants mentioned in the Bible by common and scientific name:

Acacia	*Acacia tortilis* sp.
Almond	*Amygdalus communis*
Aloe	*Aloe vera*
Apple	*Pyrus malus*
Balm of Gilead	*Cistus incanus*
Barley	*Hordeum vulgare*
Bean	*Vicia fava*
Black cummin	*Nigella sativa*
Bramble	*Rubus sanguineus*
Broom	*Retama raetum*
Calamus	*Acorus calamus*
Caper	*Capparis spinosa*
Carob	*Ceratonia siliqua*
Cassia, cinnamon	*Cinnamomum aromaticum*
Cedar	*Cedrus libani*
Coriander	*Coriandrum sativum*
Cotton	*Gossypium* sp.
Cumin	*Cuminum cyminum*

Cypress	*Cupressus sempervirens*
Dill	*Anethum graveolens*
Ebony	*Diospyros ebenum*
Fig	*Ficus carica*
Flax	*Linum ustitatissimum*
Frankincense	*Boswellia* sp.
Galbanum	*Ferula galbaniflua*
Gall	*Conium maculatum*
Garlic	*Allium sativum*
Gourd	*Citrullus colycinthus*
Grape	*Vitis vinifera*
Gum resin	*Pistacia palaestina*
Henna	*Lawsonia inermis*
Hyssop	*Origanum syriacum*
Laurel	*Laurus nobilis*
Leek	*Allium porrum*
Lentil	*Lens culinaris*
Lign aloe	*Aquilaria malaccensis*
Lily of the field	*Anemone coronaria*
Mandrake	*Mandragora autumnalis*
Melon	*Citrullus lanatus*
Millet	*Sorghum vulgare*
Mint	*Mentha longifolia*

Mustard	*Brassica nigra*
Myrrh	*Commiphora gileadensis*
Myrtle	*Myrtus communis*
Nettle	*Urtica pilulifera*
Oak	*Quercus calliprinos*
Olive	*Olea europaea*
Onion	*Allium cepa*
Palm	*Phoenix dactylifera*
Papyrus	*Cyperus papyrus*
Pine	*Pinus halepensis*
Pink Rockrose	*Cistus incanus*
Pistachio	*Pistacia vera*
Plane tree	*Platanus orientalis*
Pomegranate	*Punica granatum*
Poplar	*Populus euphratica*
Reed	*Phragmites australis*
Rose of Sharon	*Gladiolus italicus*
Rue	*Ruta chalepensis*
Rush	*Juncus maritimus*
Saffron	*Crocus sativus*
Sorghum	*Sorghum vulgare*
Spikenard	*Nardostachys jatamansi*
Stone pine	*Pinus pinaea*

Styrax	*Styrax officinalis*
Sycamore	*Ficus sycomorus*
Tamarisk	*Tamarix aphylla*
Tares	*Cephalaria syriaca*
Terebinth	*Pistacia atlantica*
Thistle	*Gundelia tournefortii*
Thorn	*Sarcopoterium spinosum*
Thyine wood	*Tetraclinis articulata*
Walnut	*Juglans regia*
Wheat	*Triticum aestivum*
Willow	*Salix alba*
Wormwood	*Artemisia herba-alba*
Yeast	*Saccharomyces cerivisae*